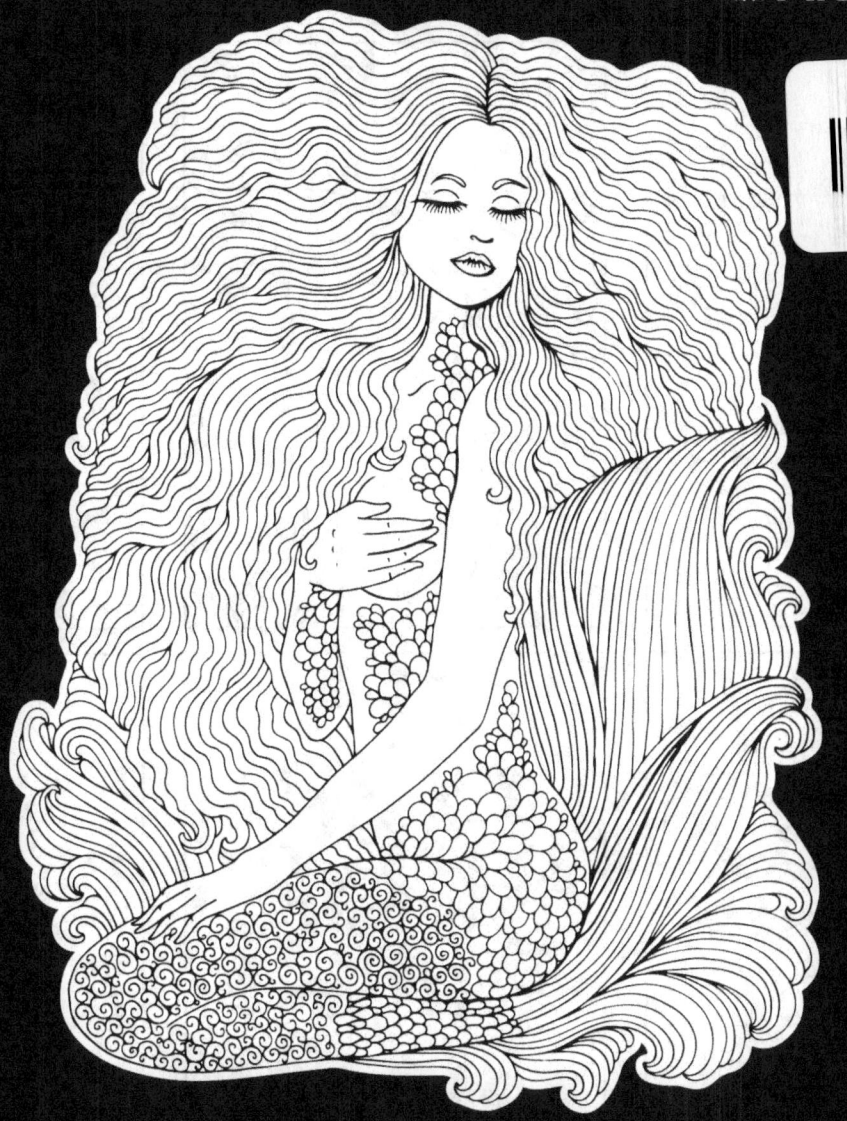

MERMAID
COLORING BOOK
FOR ADULTS

Preview of Coloring Pages

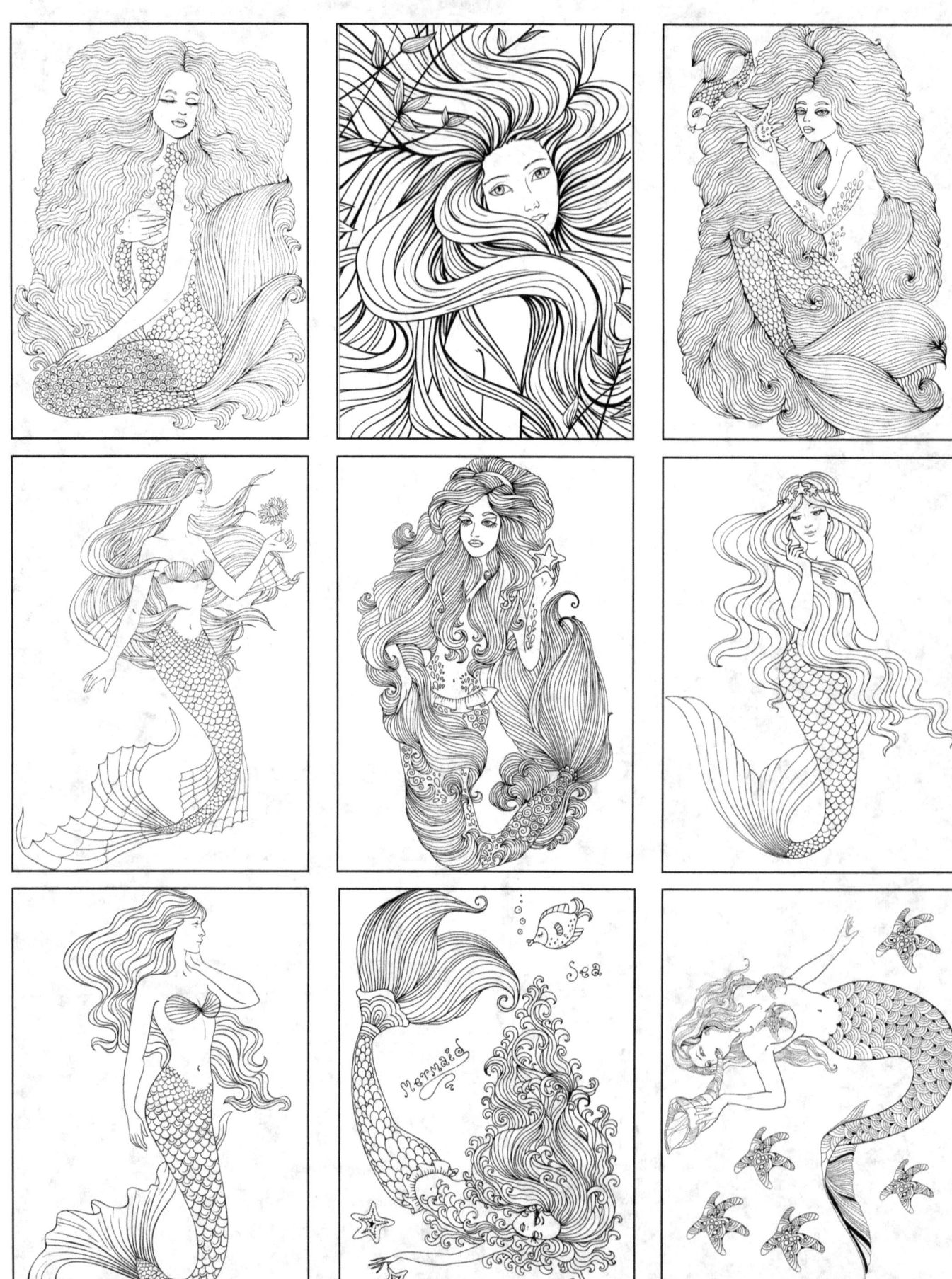

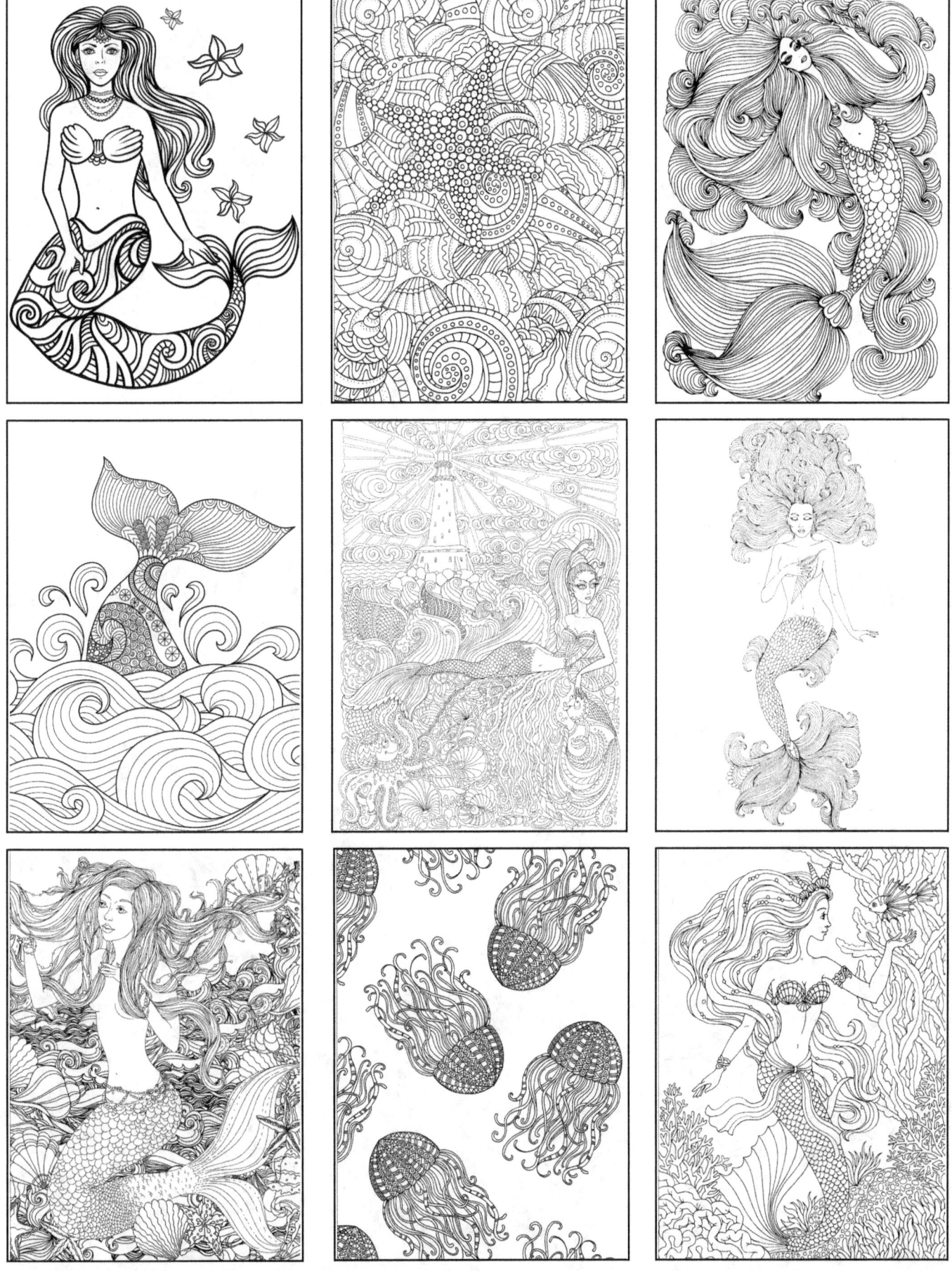

Preview of Coloring Pages

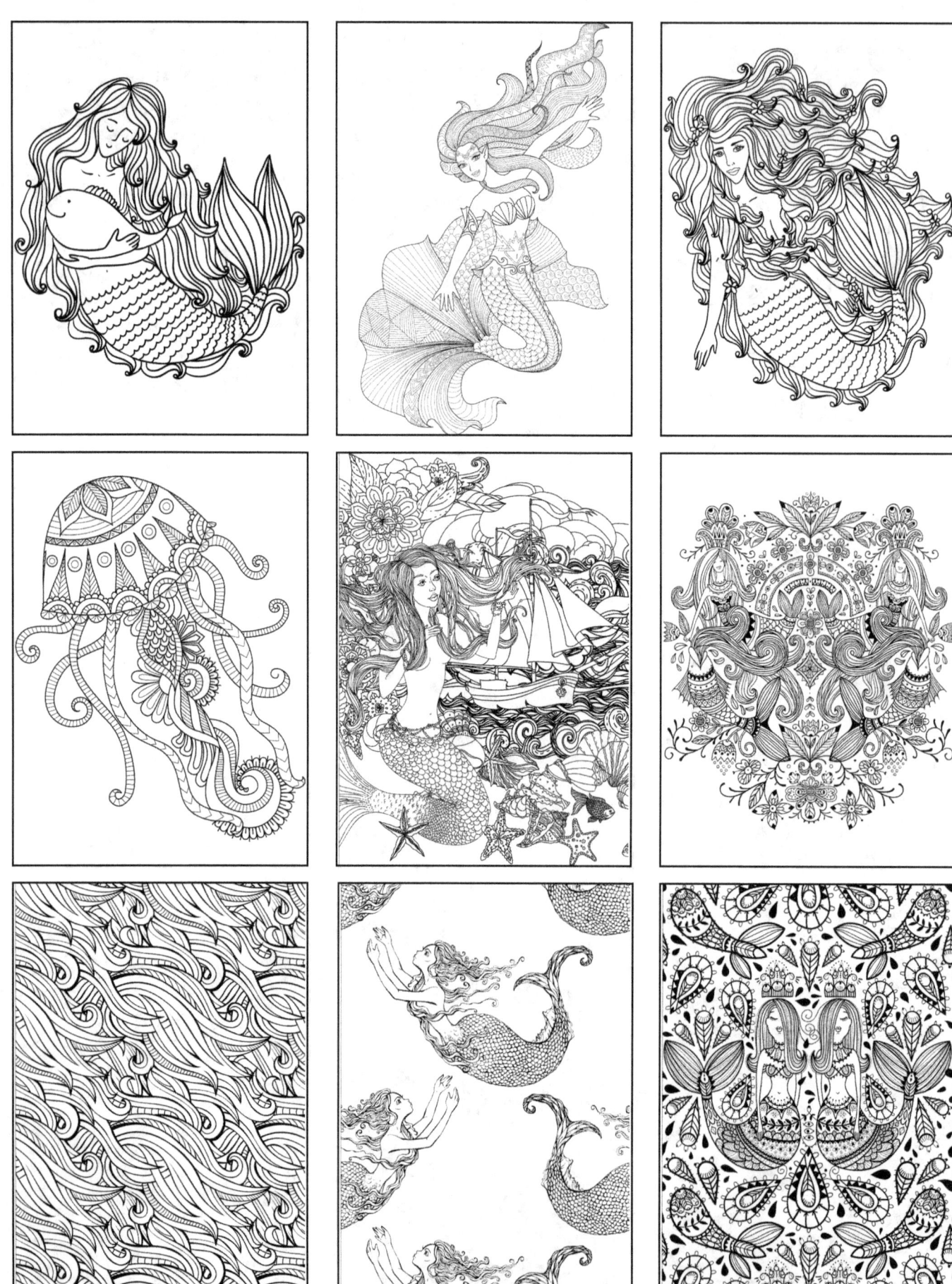

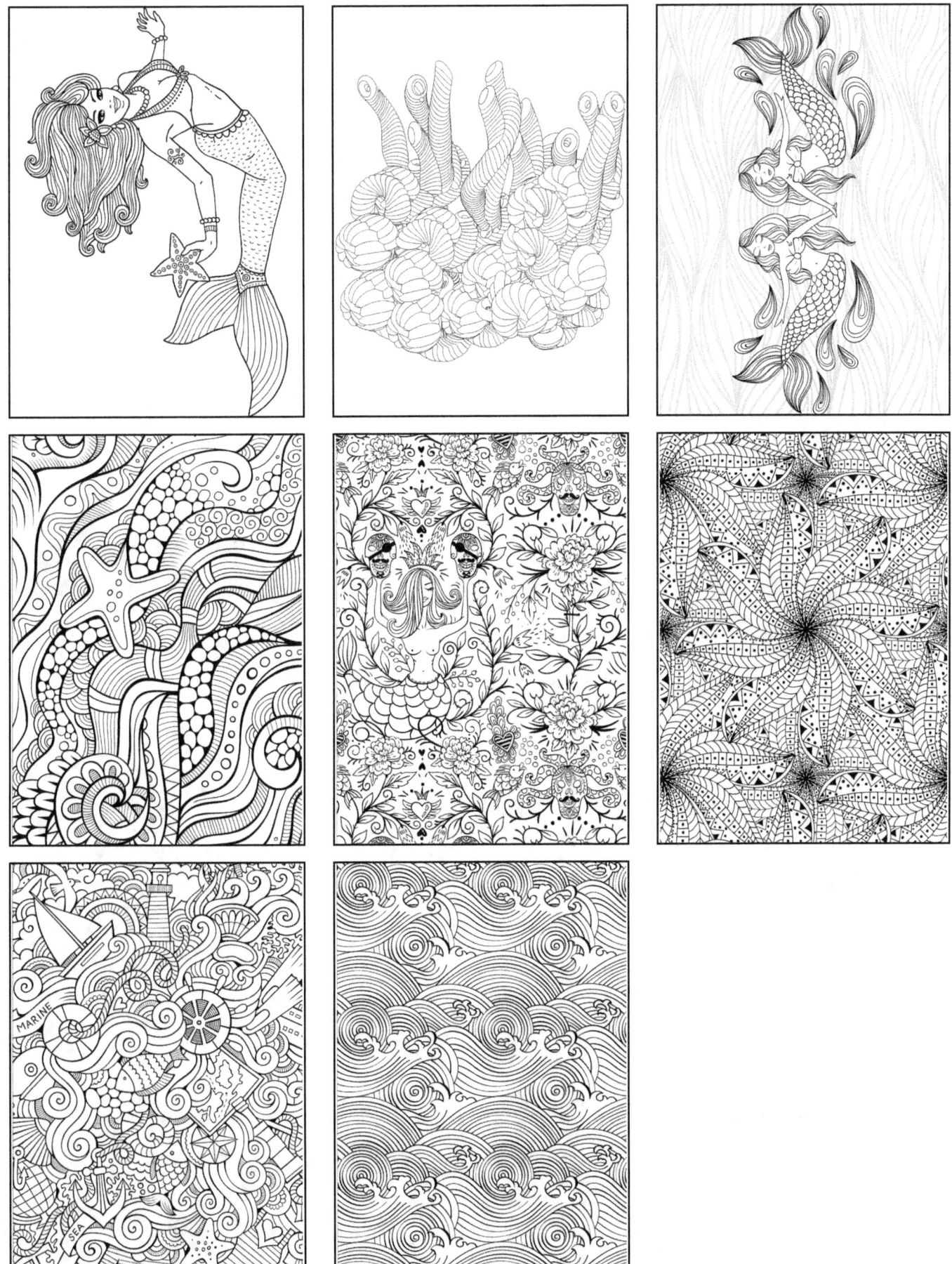

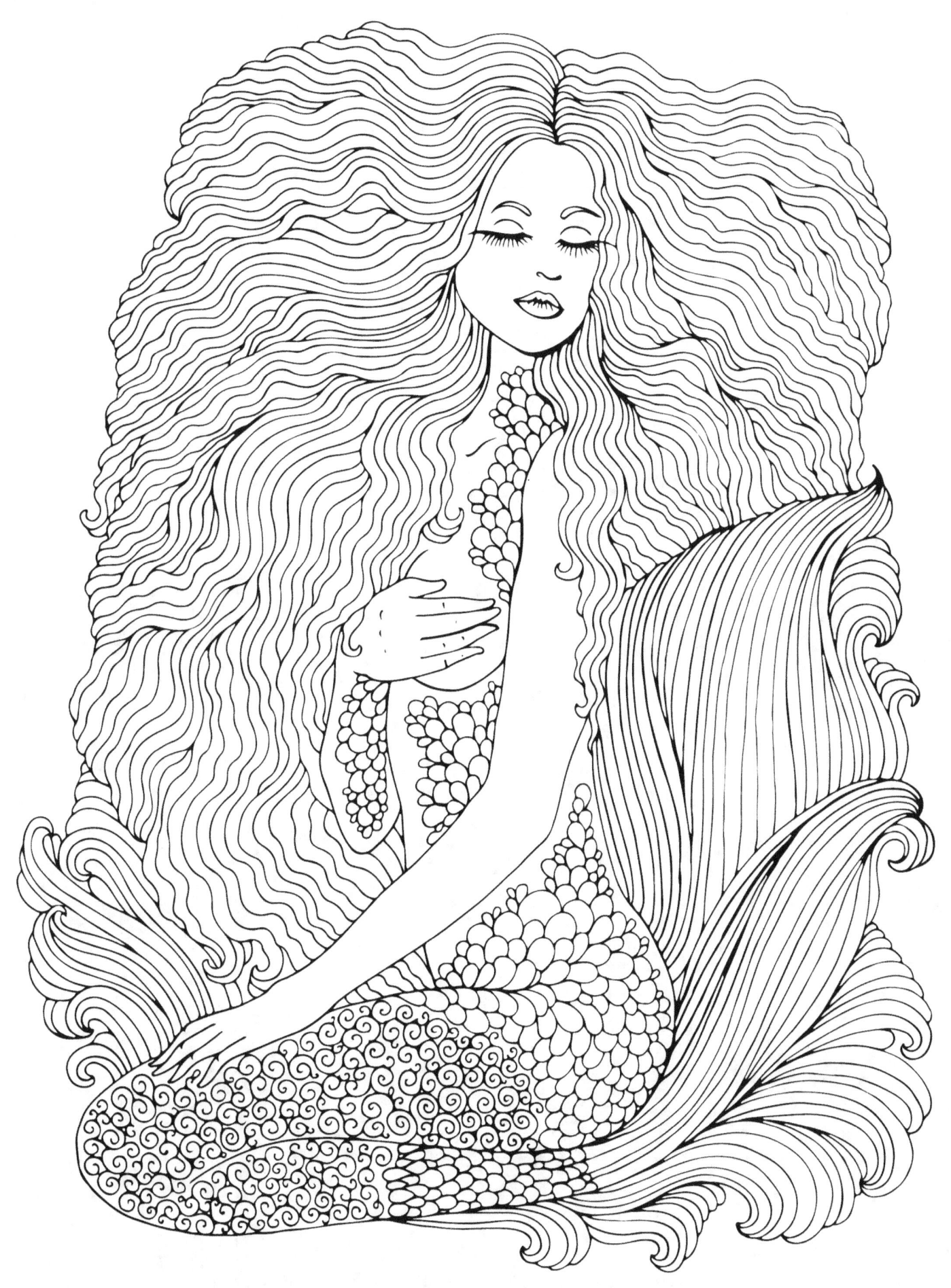

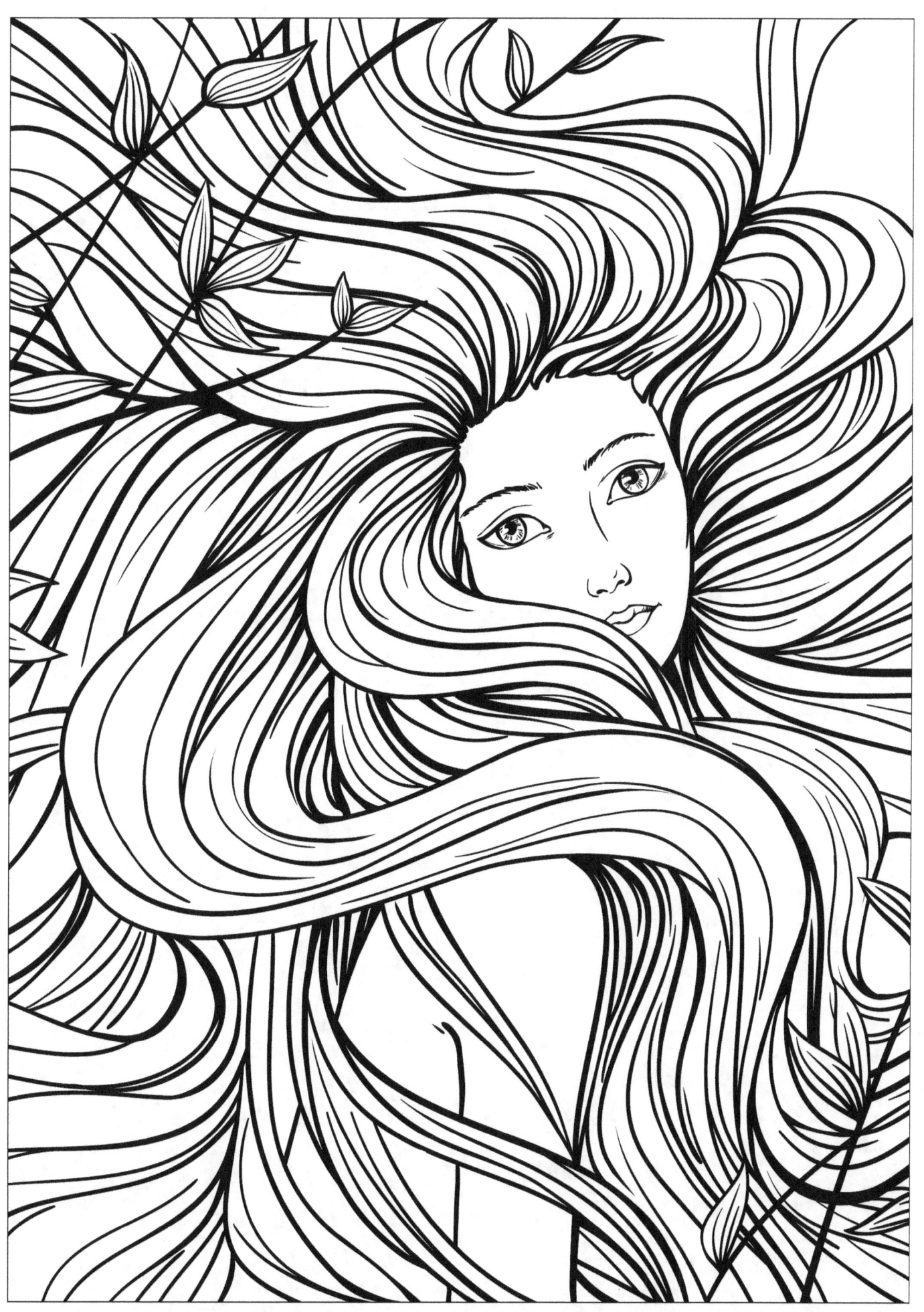

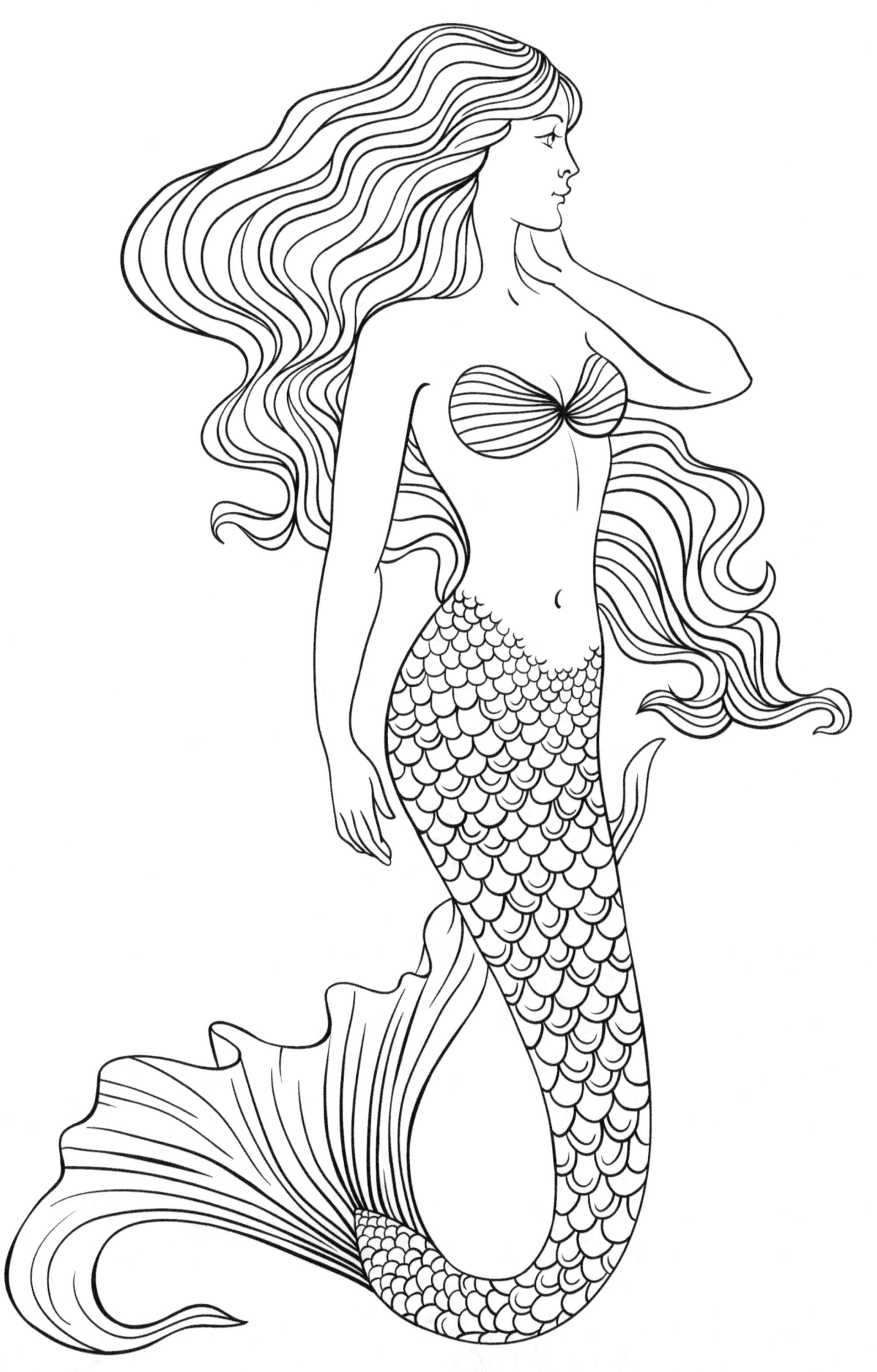

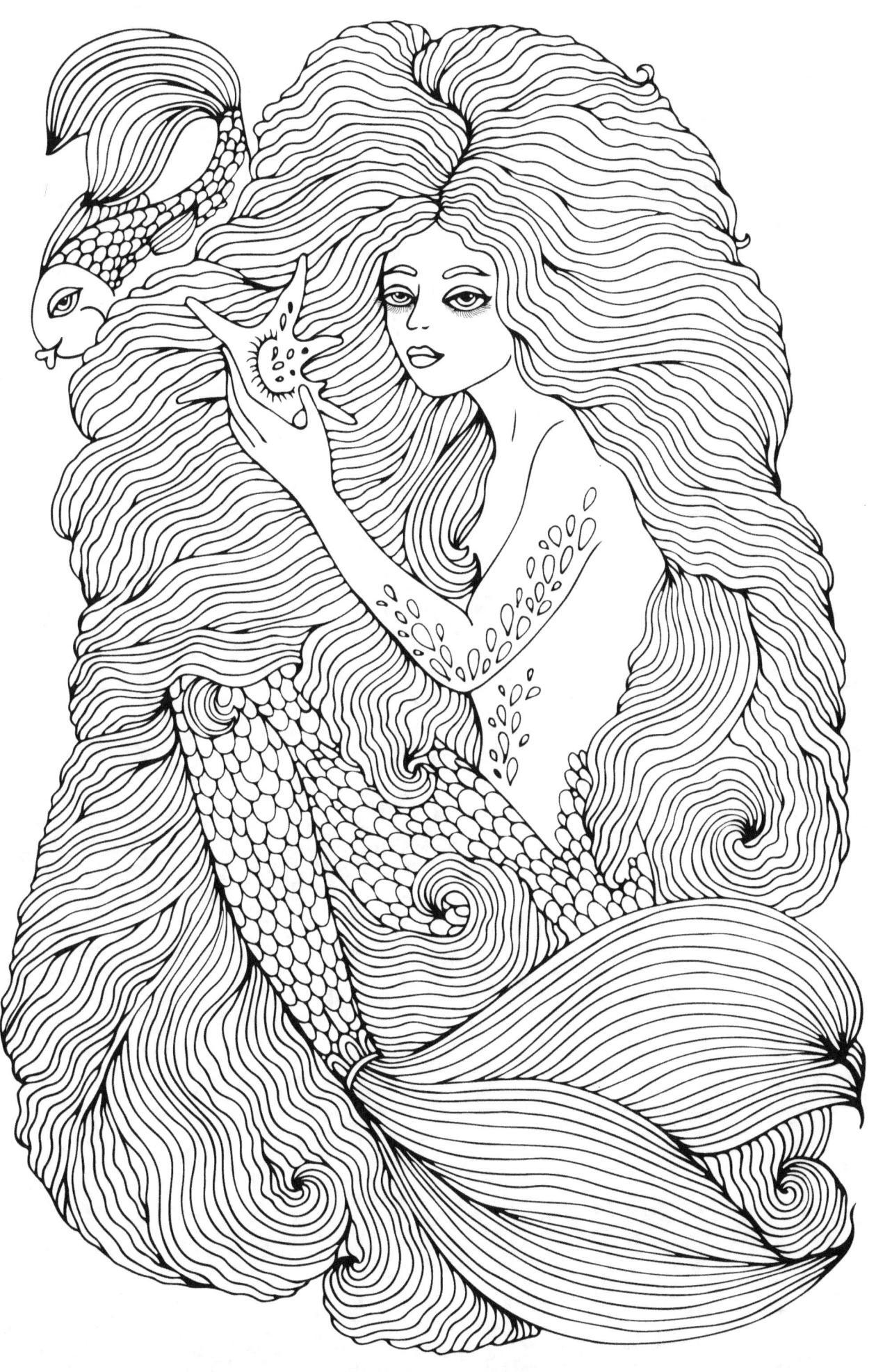

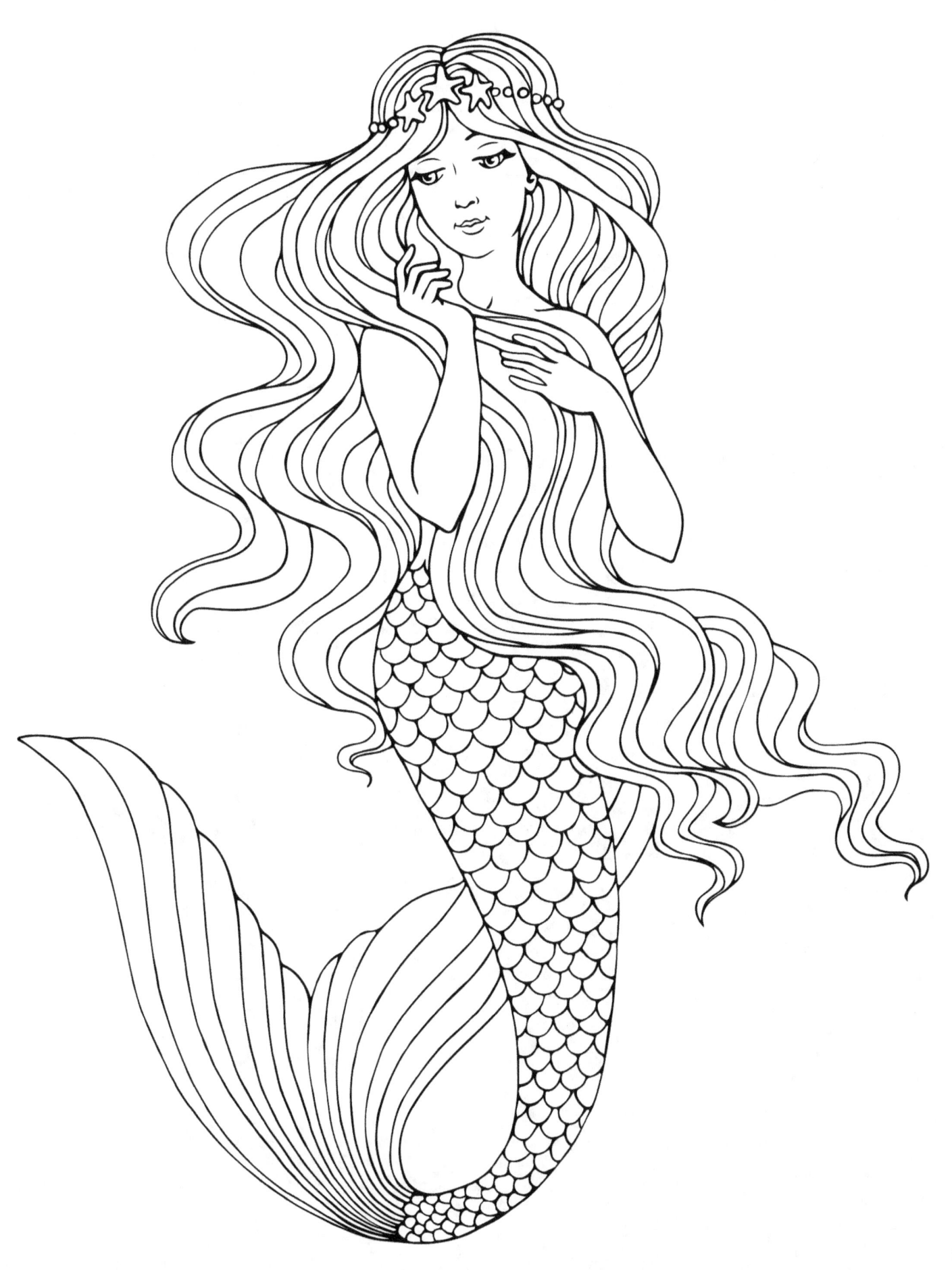

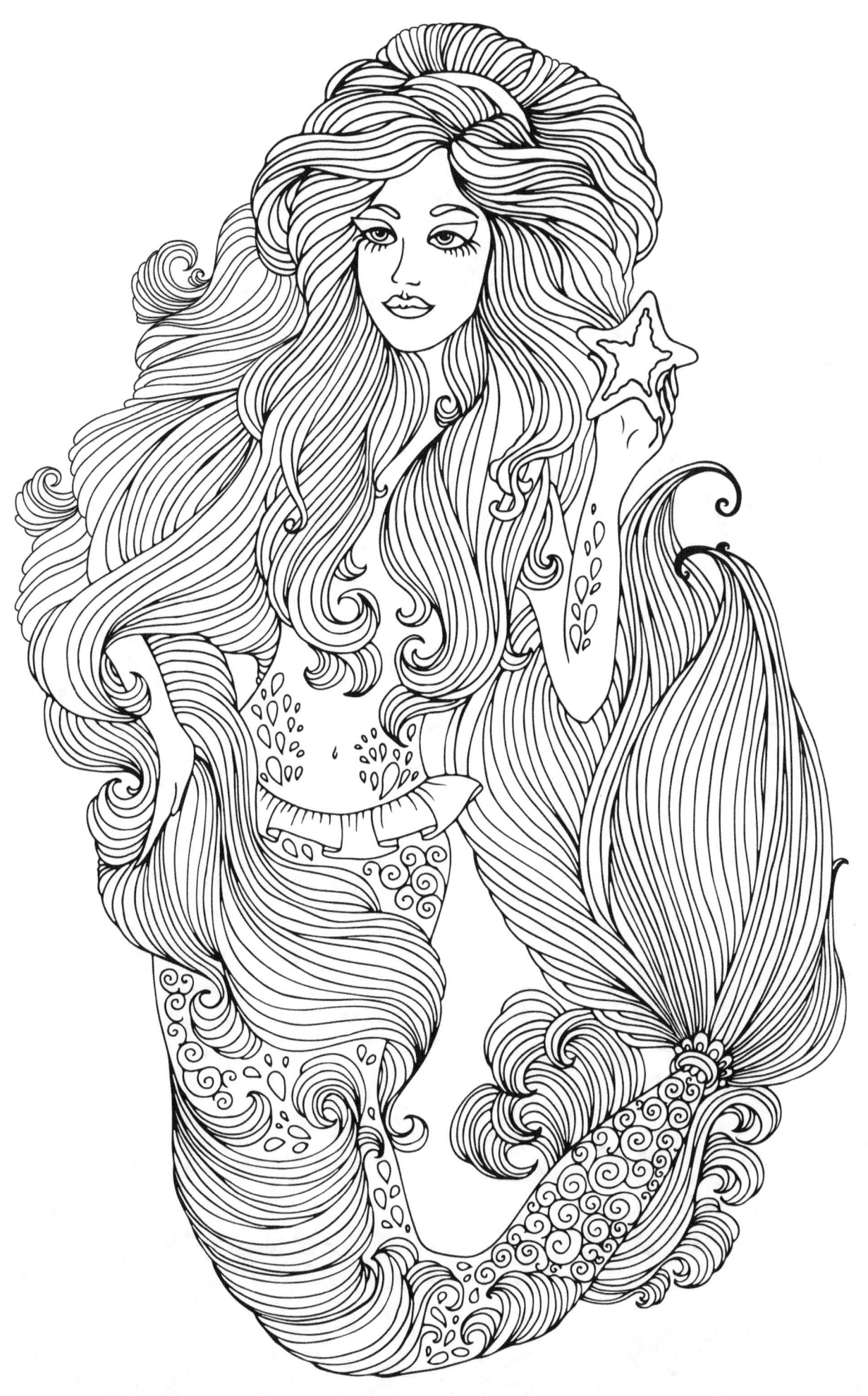

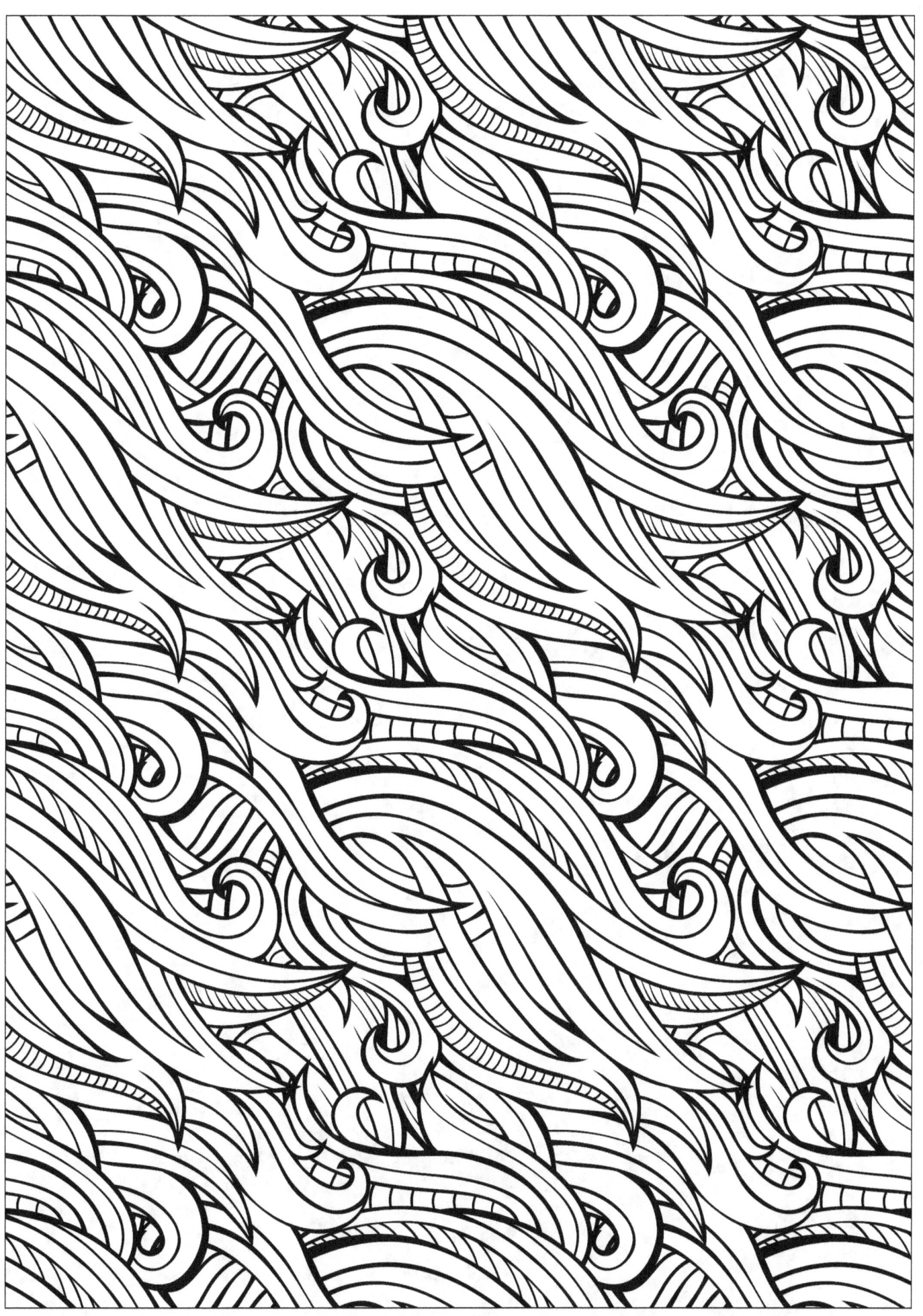

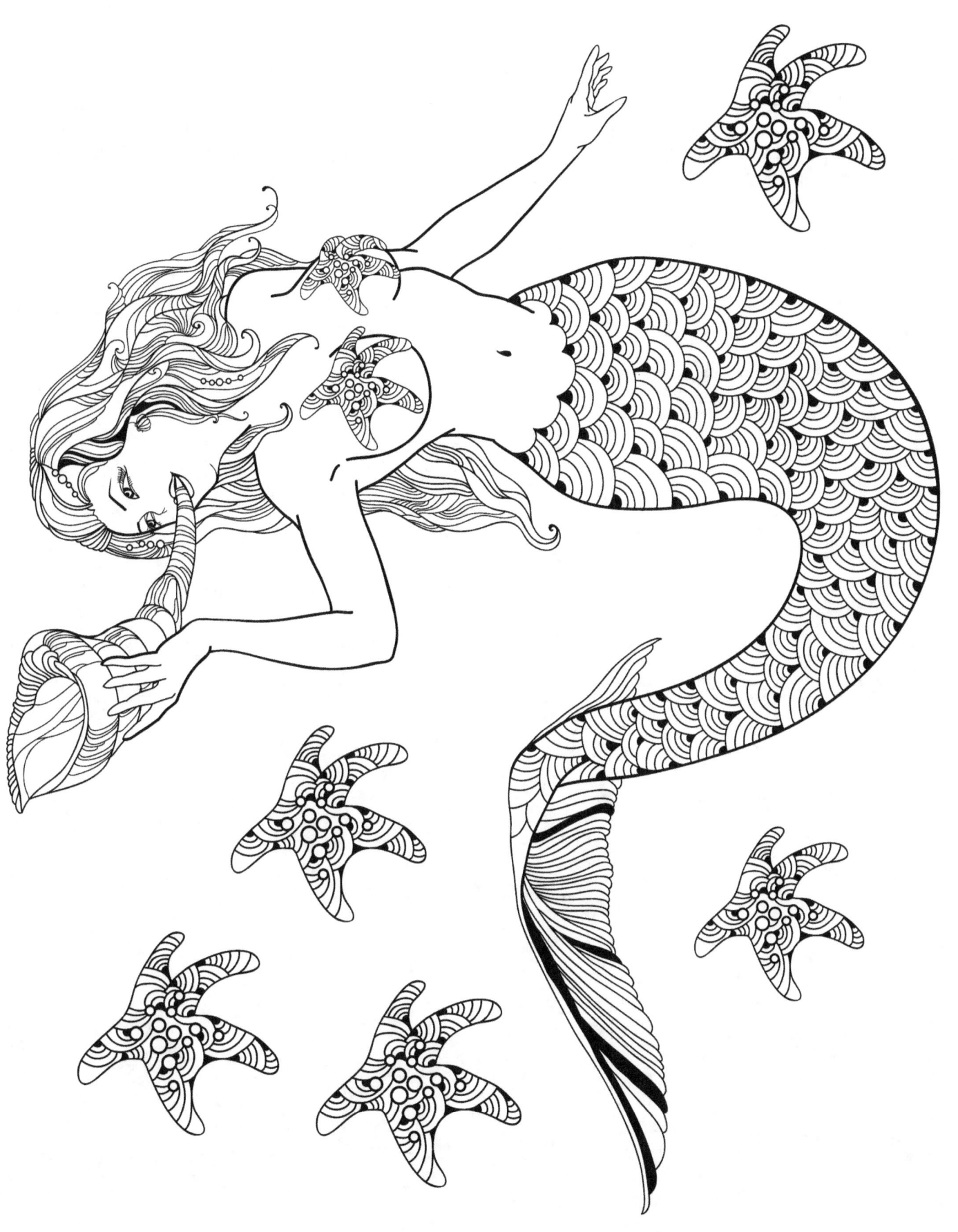

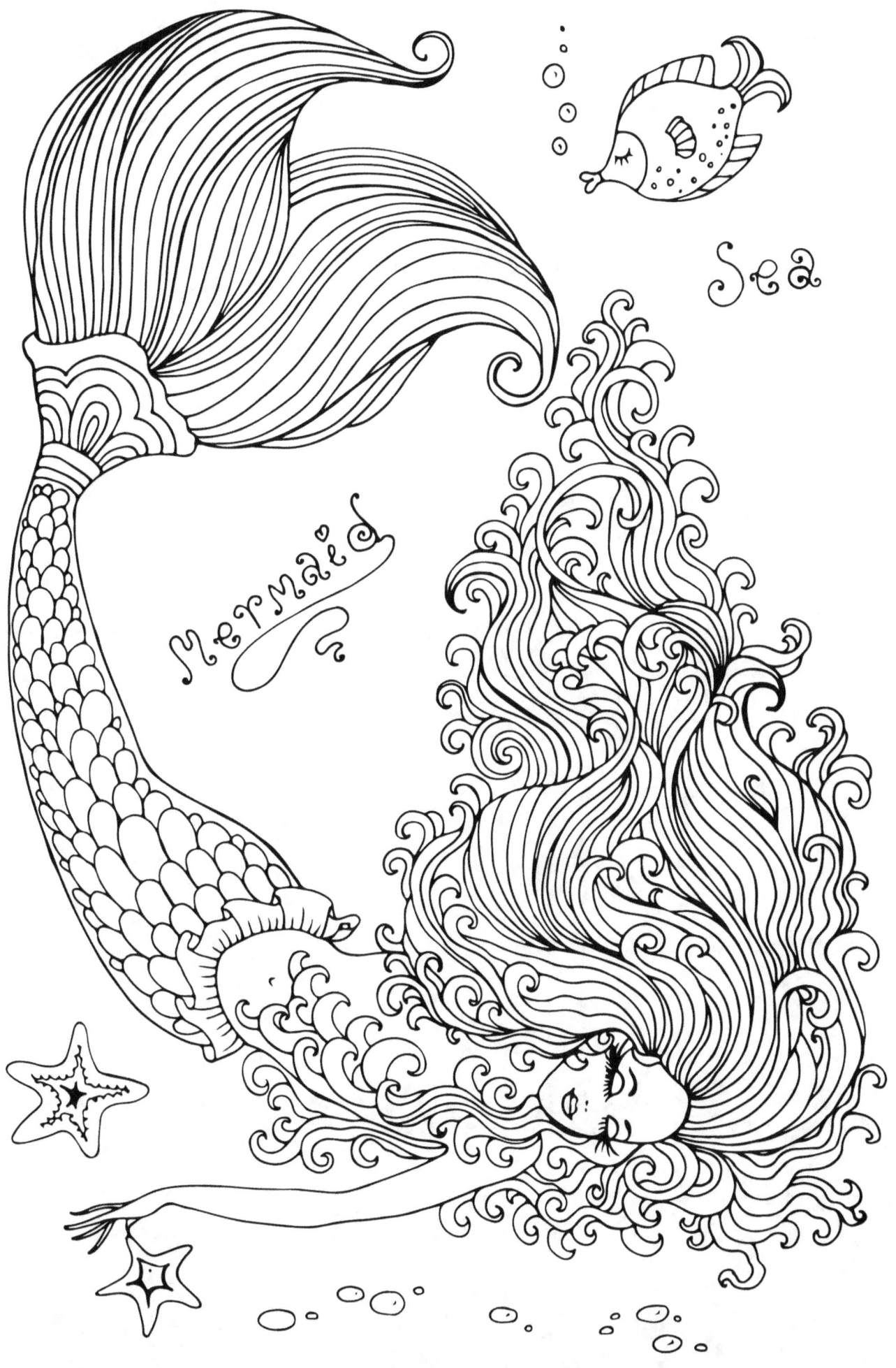

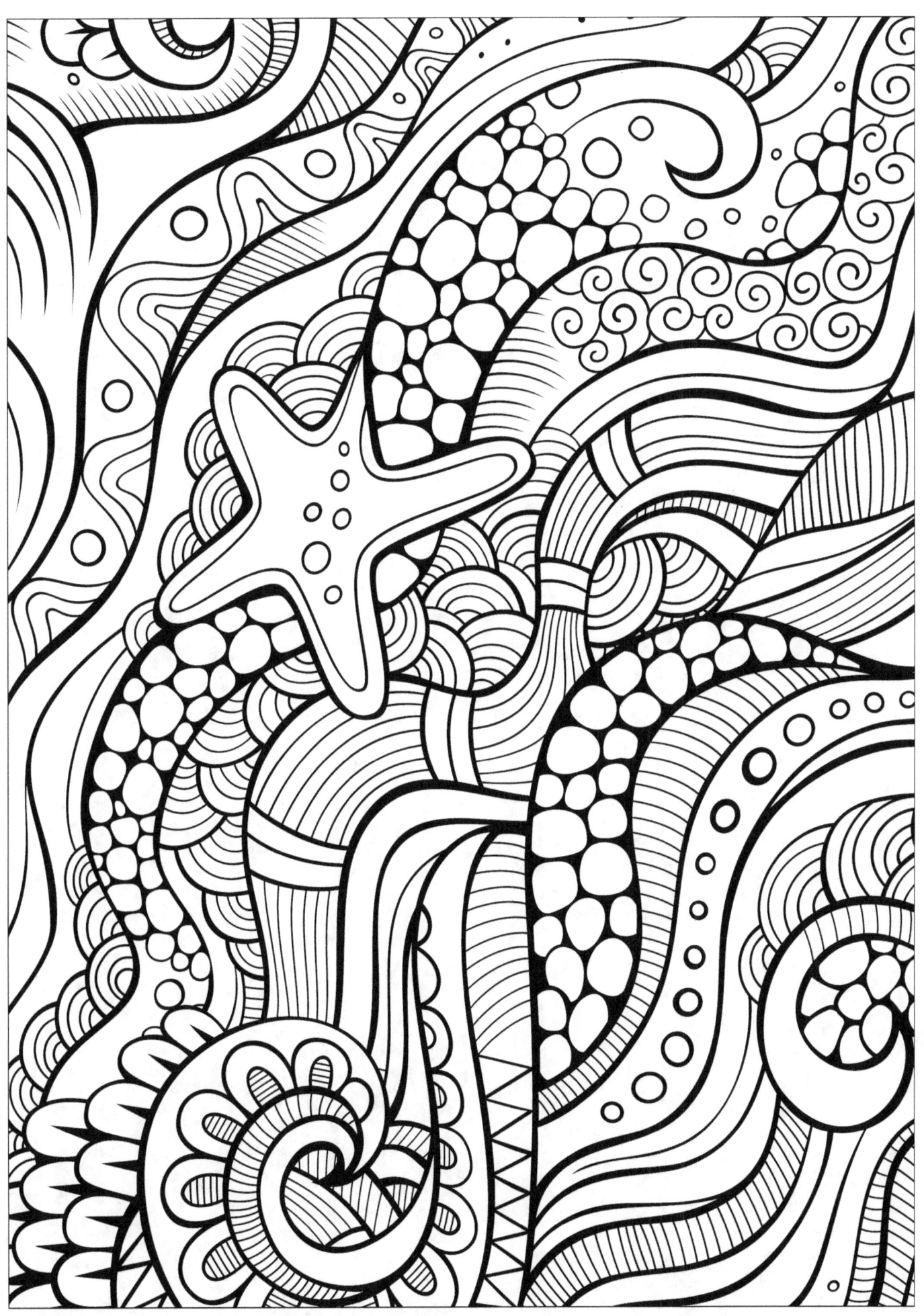

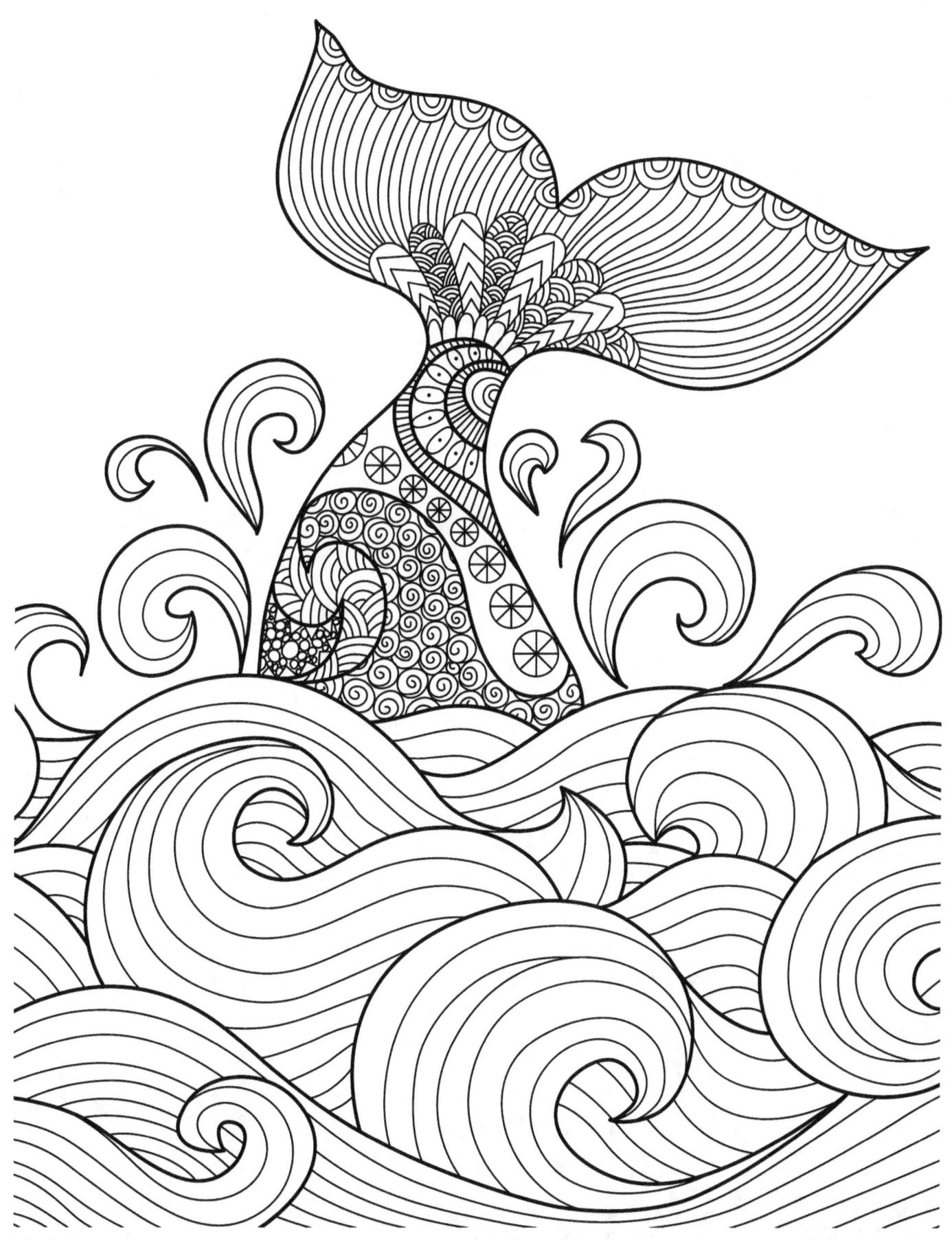

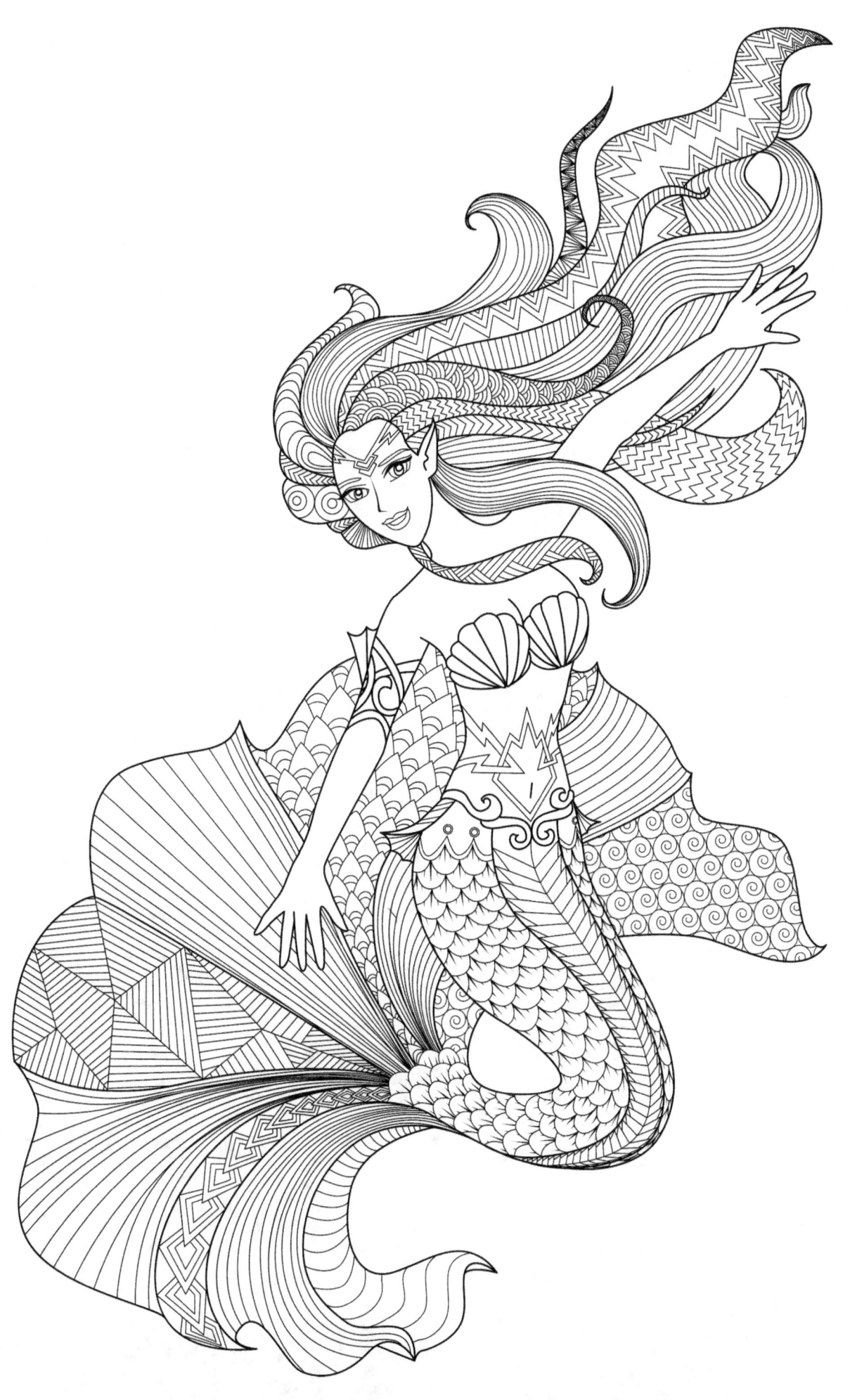

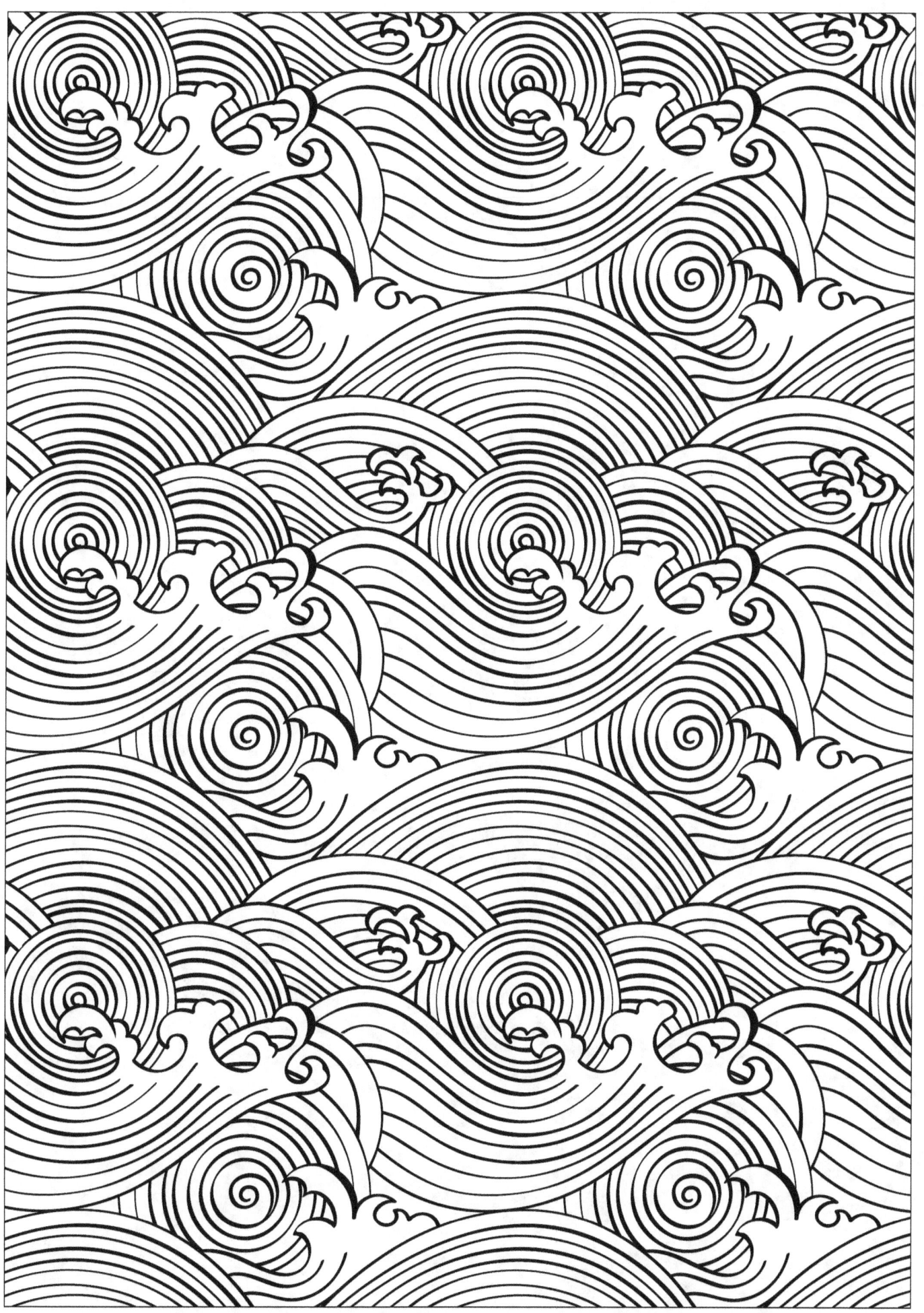

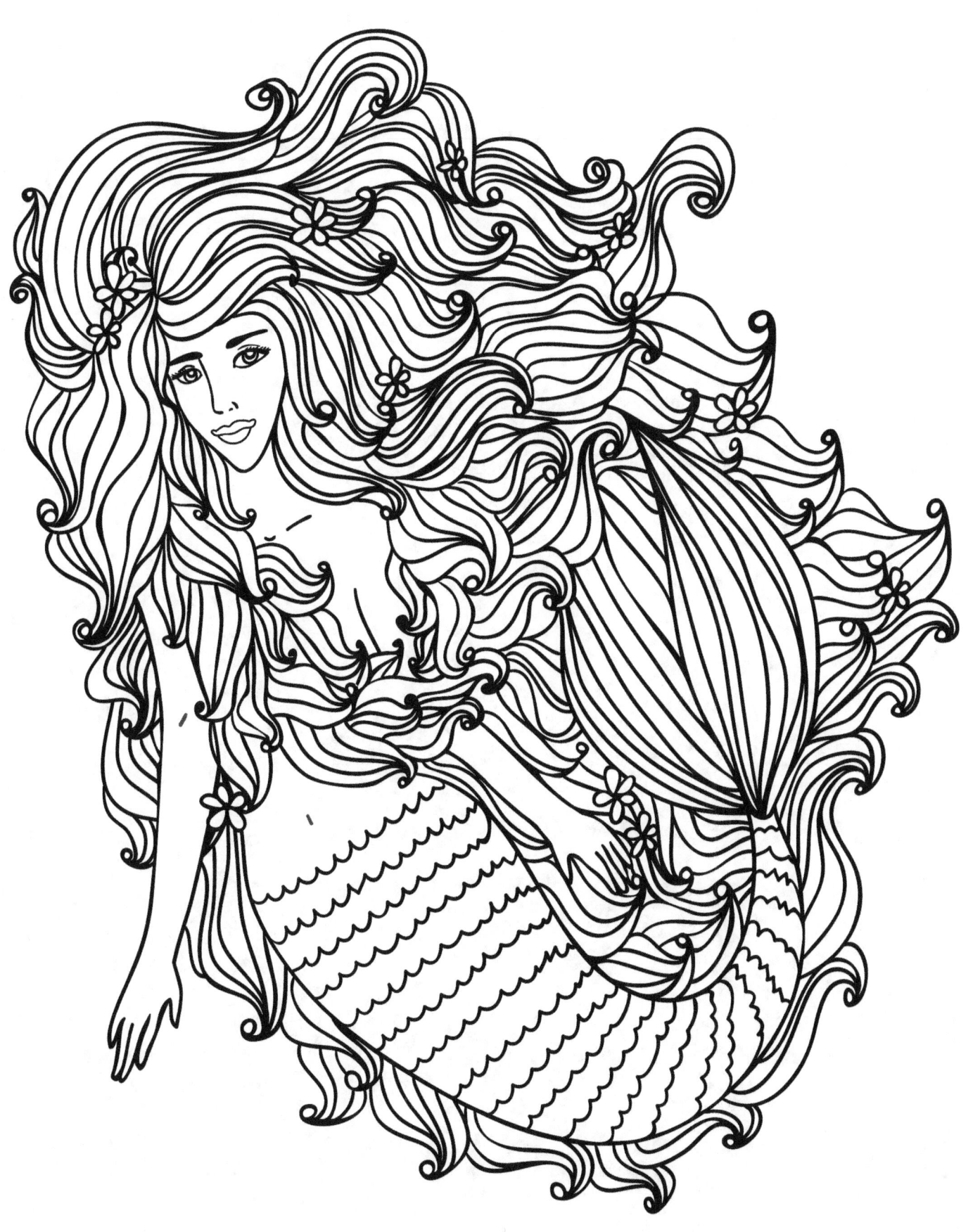

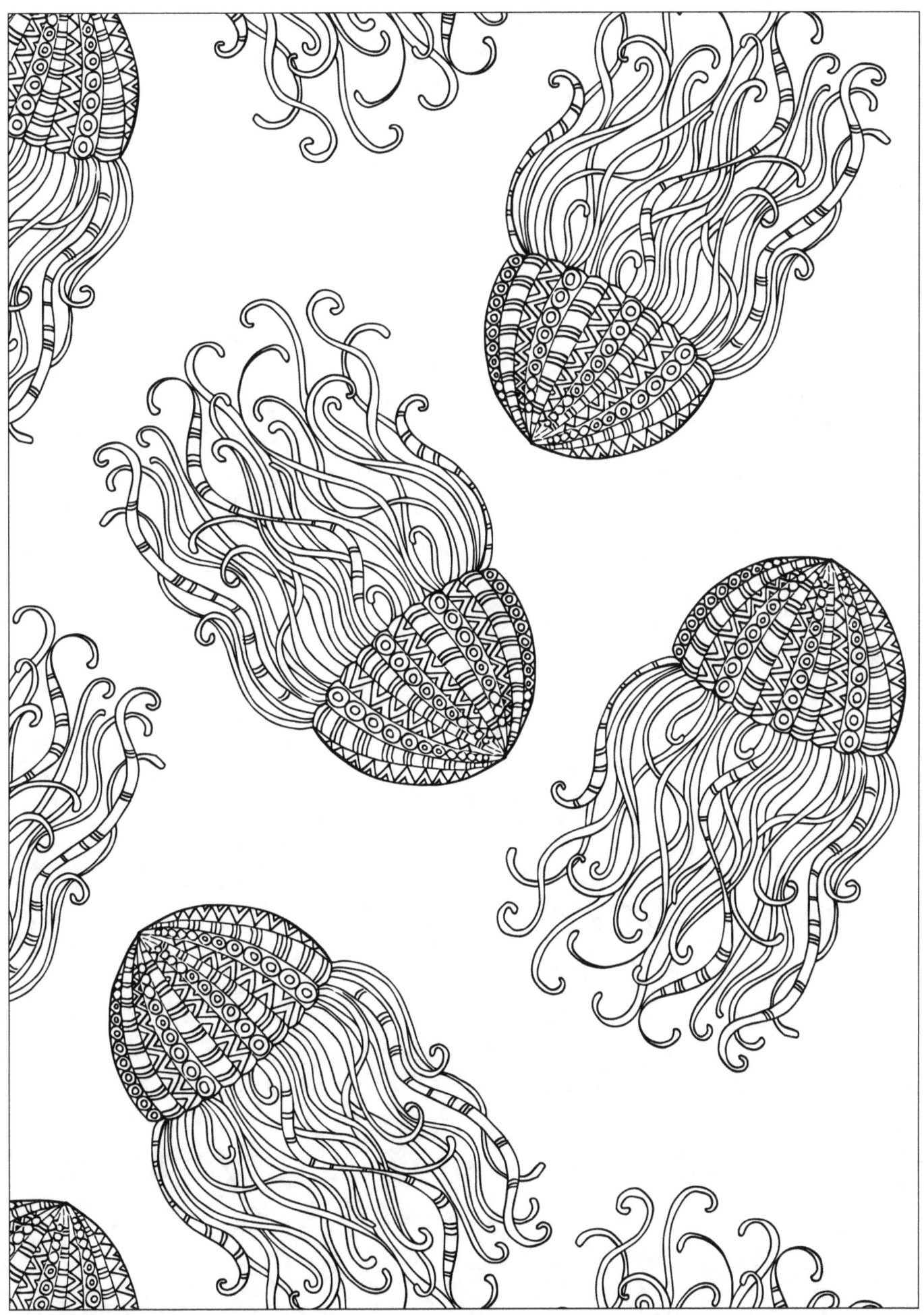

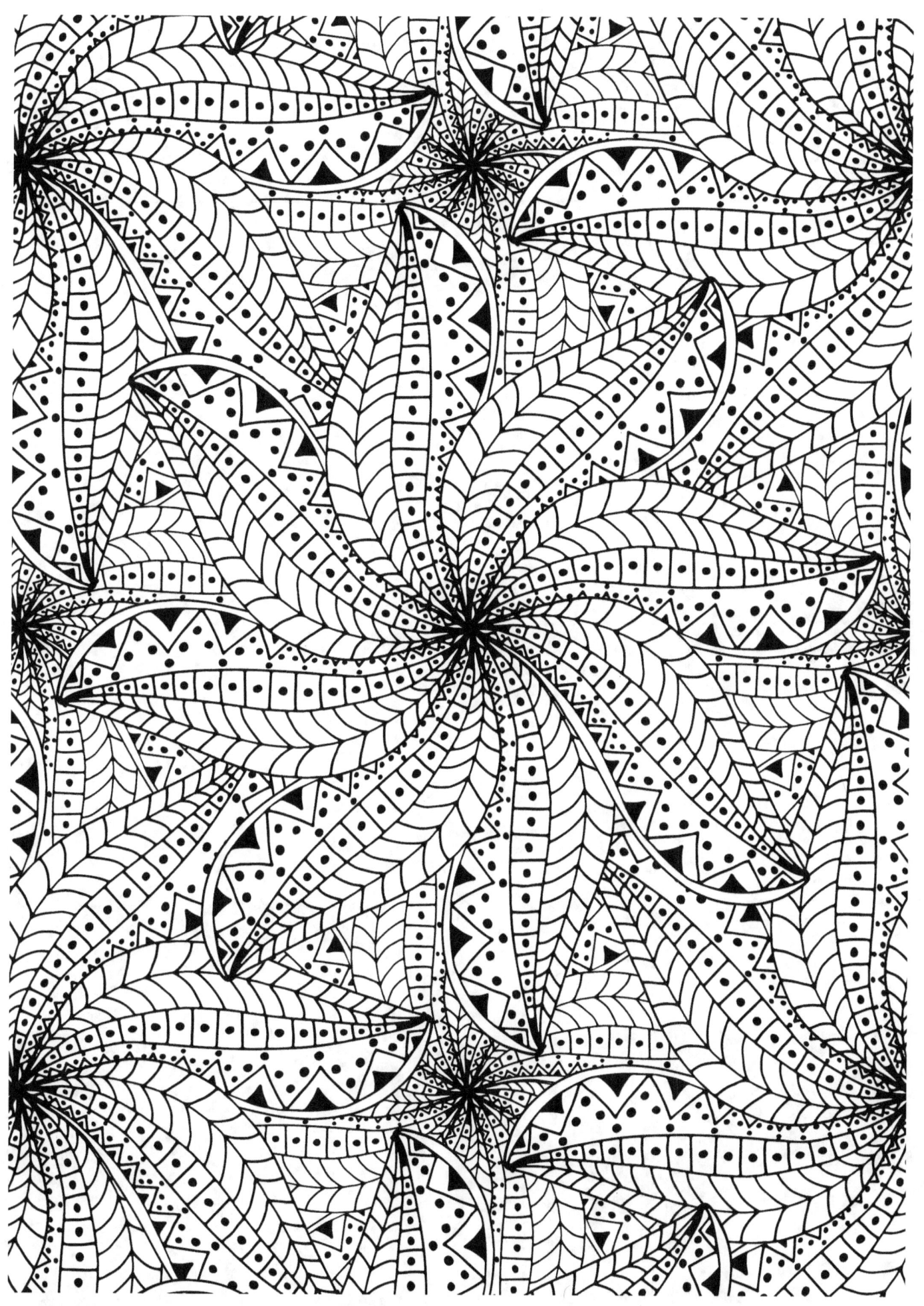

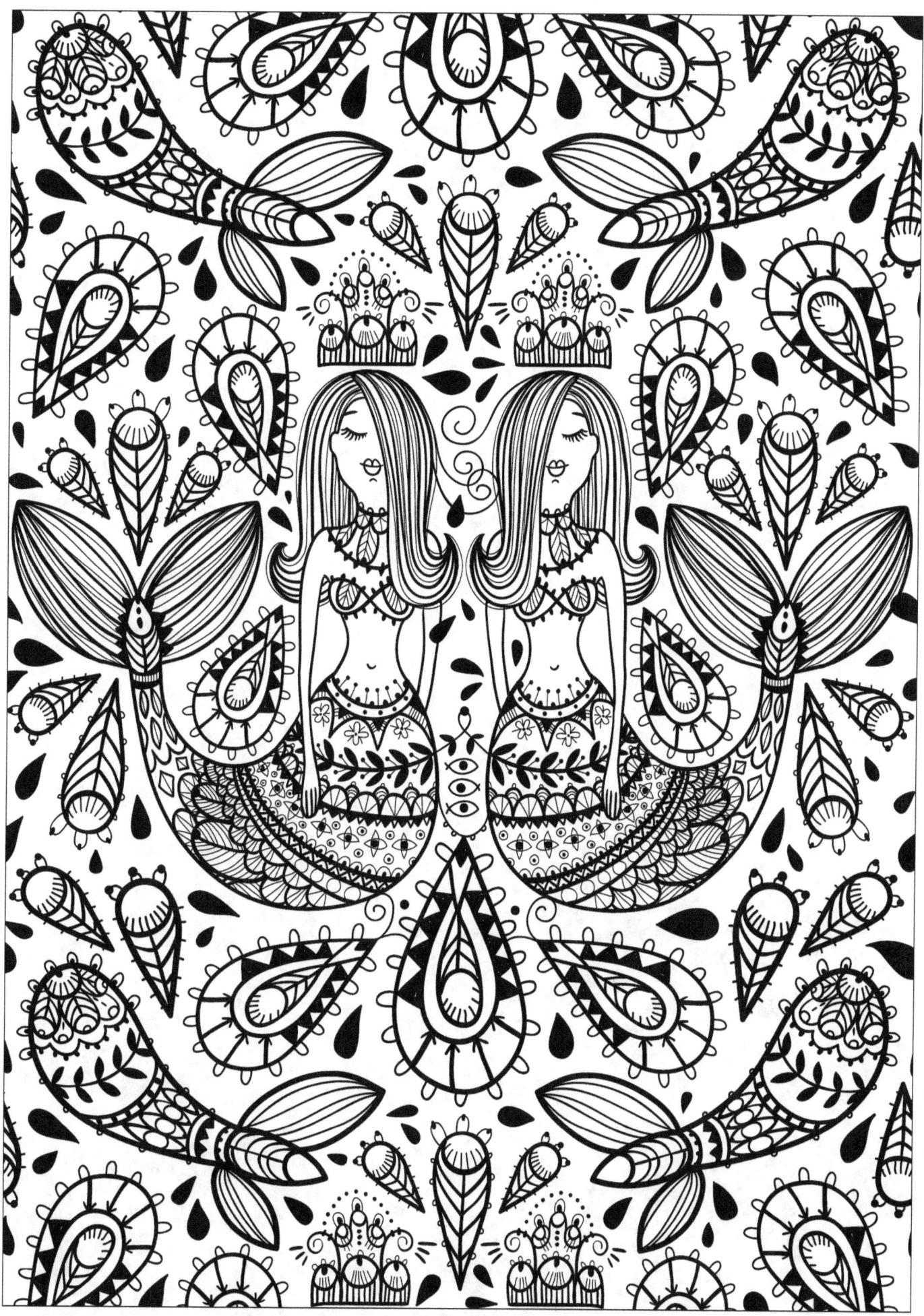

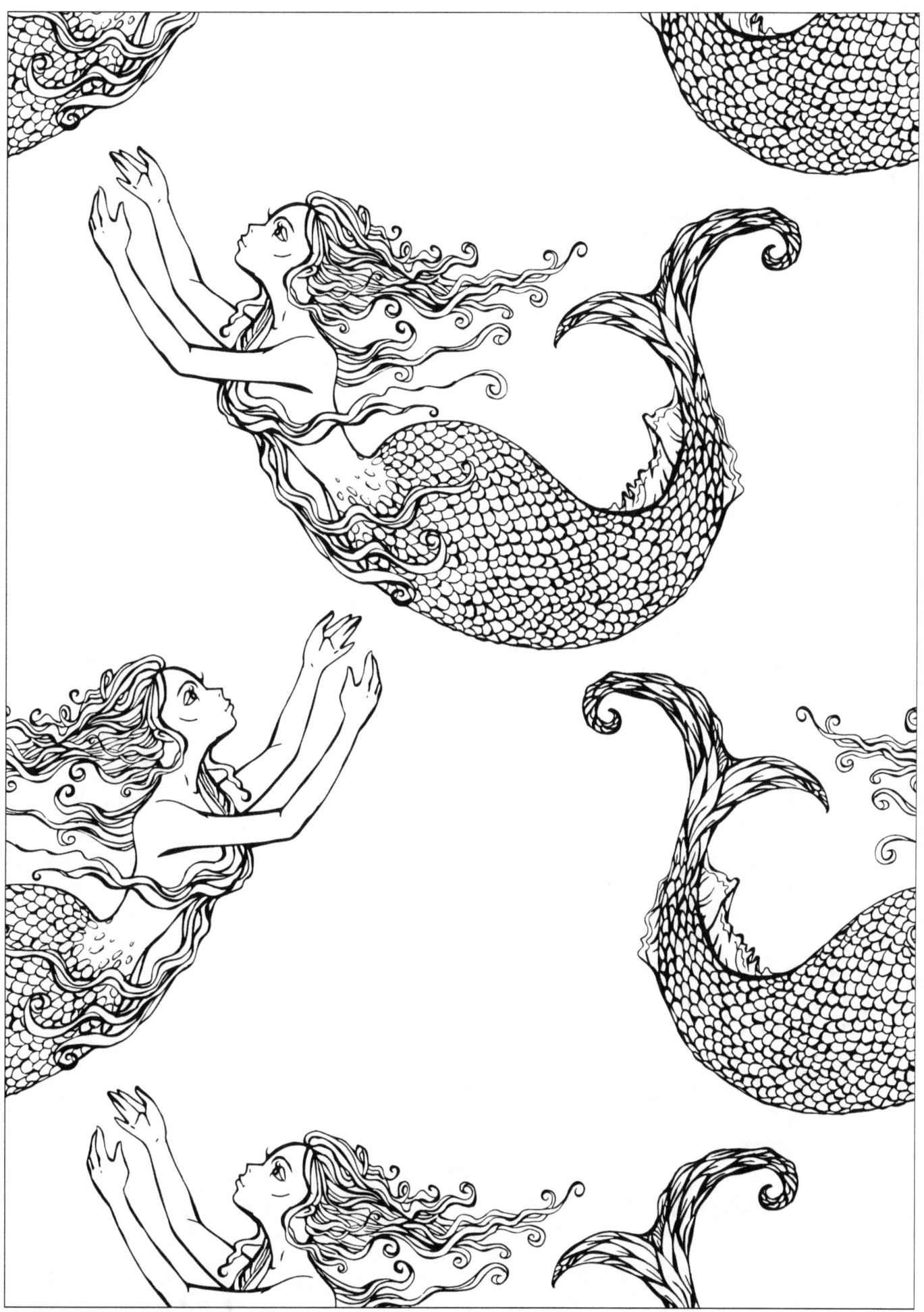

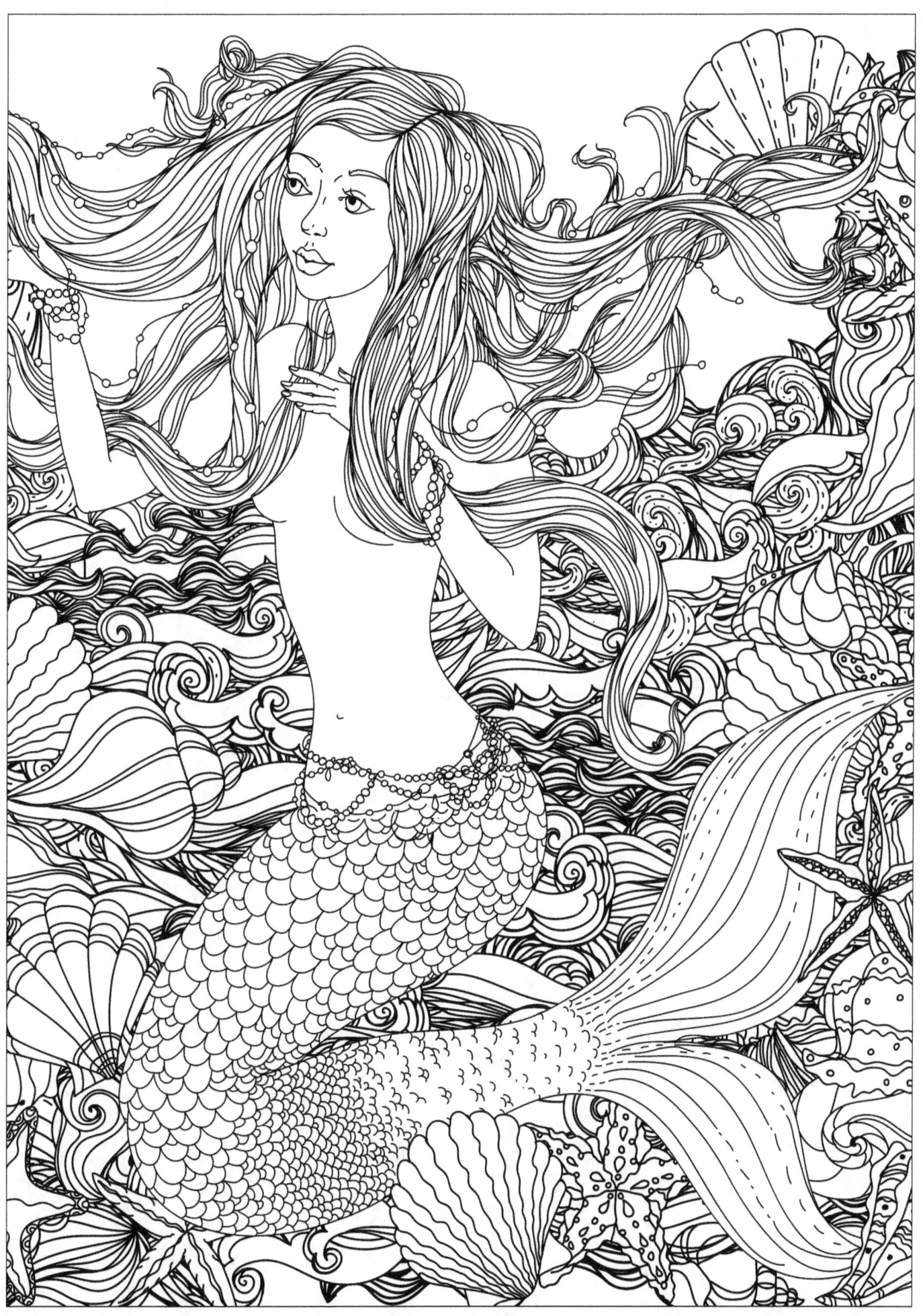

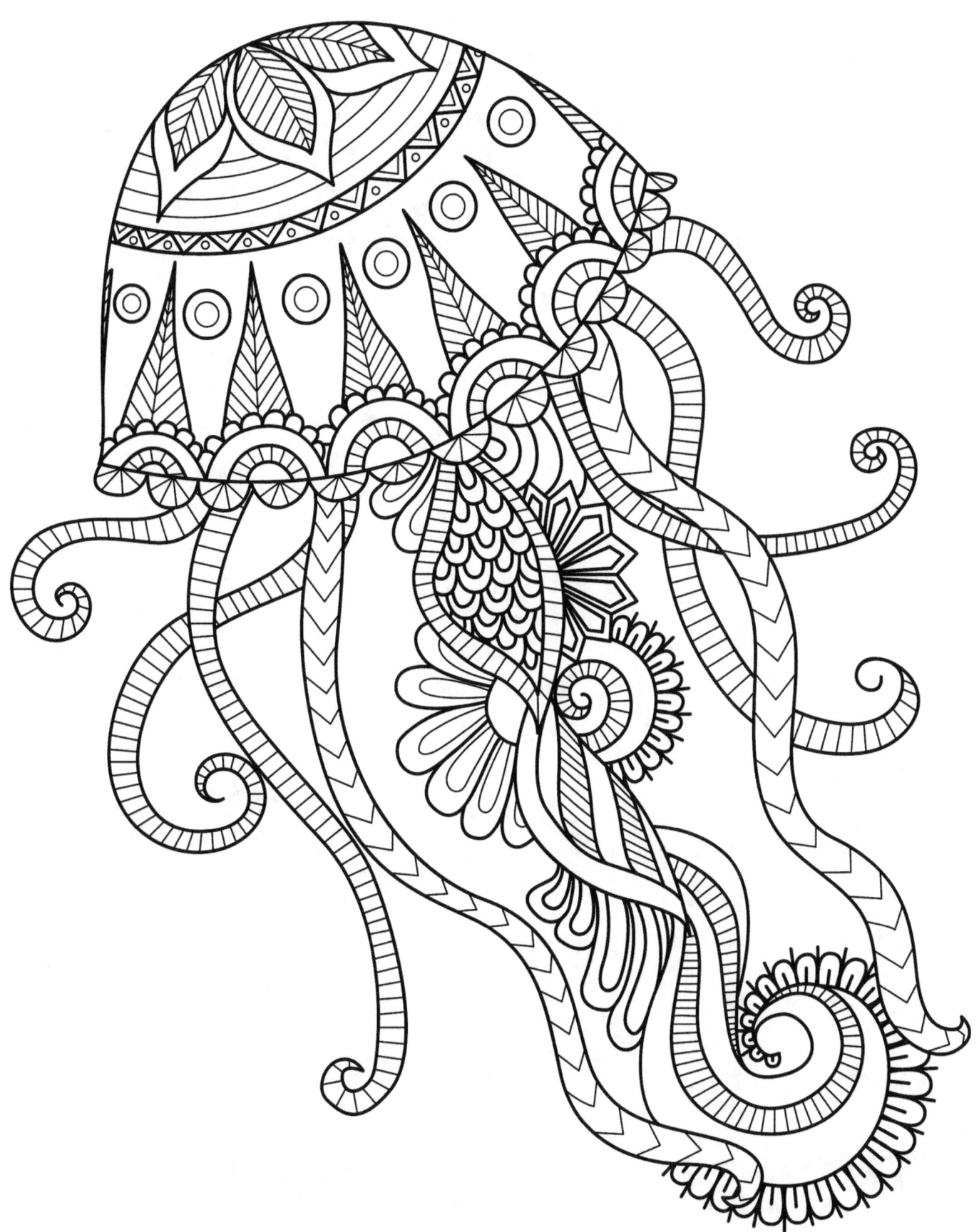

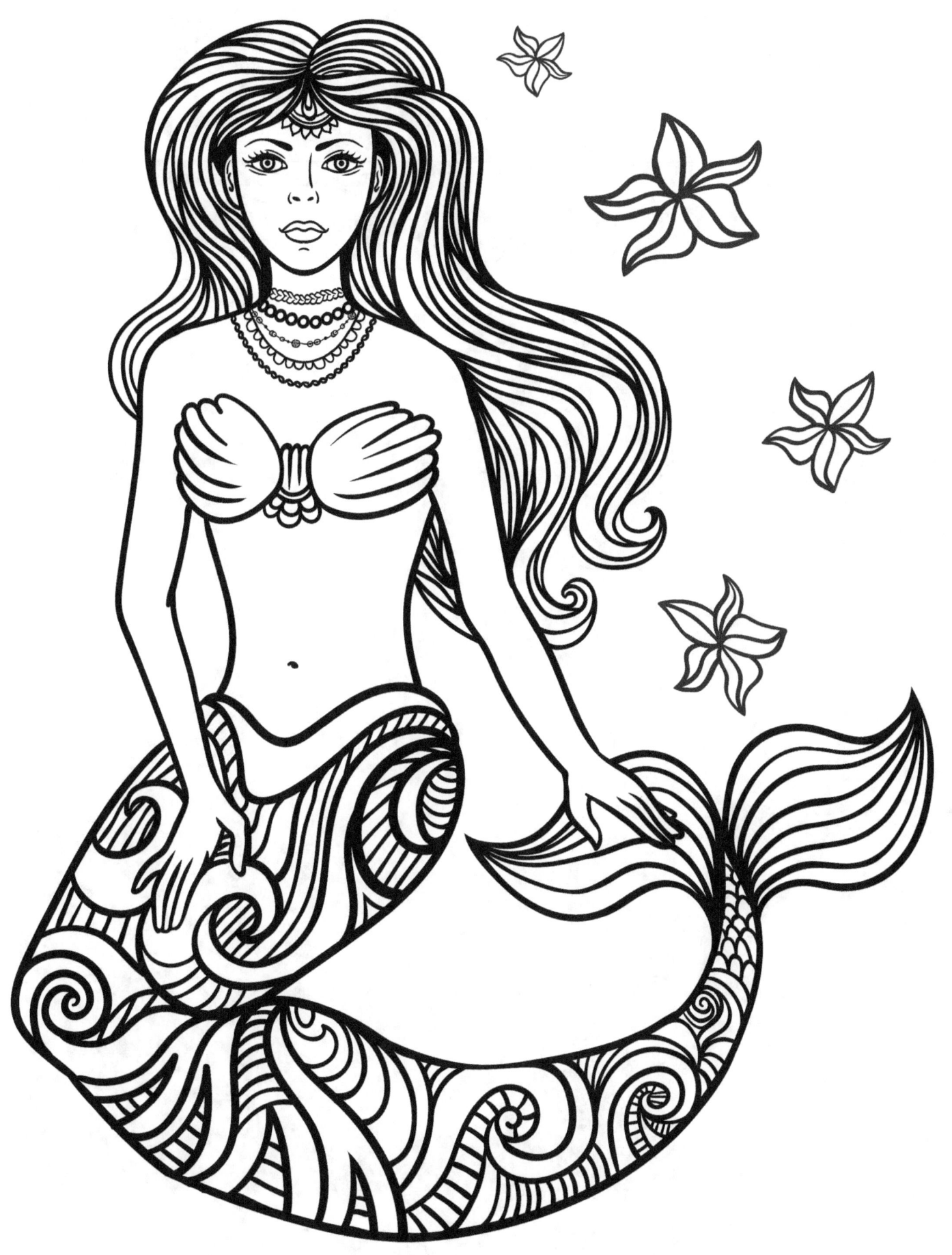

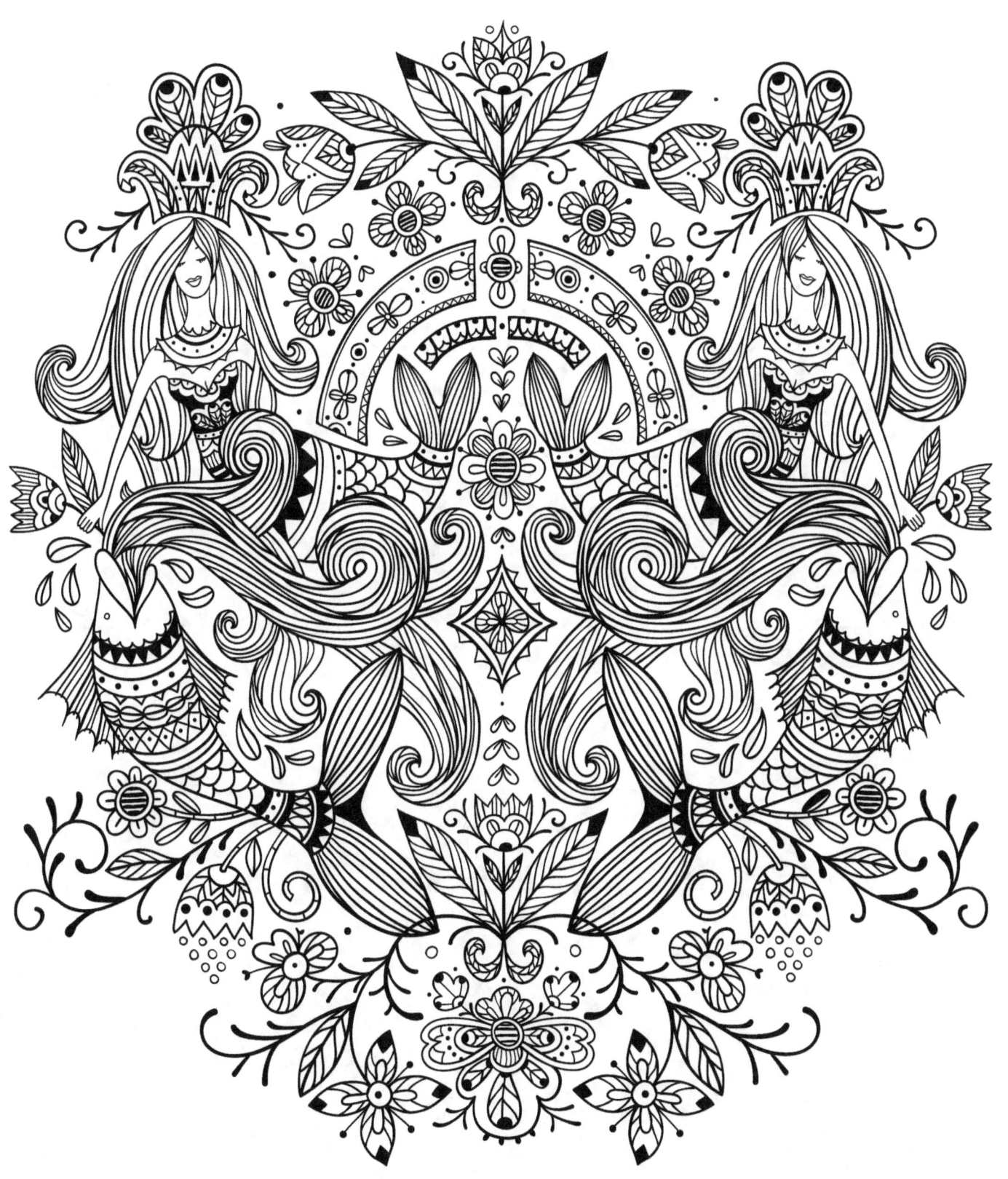

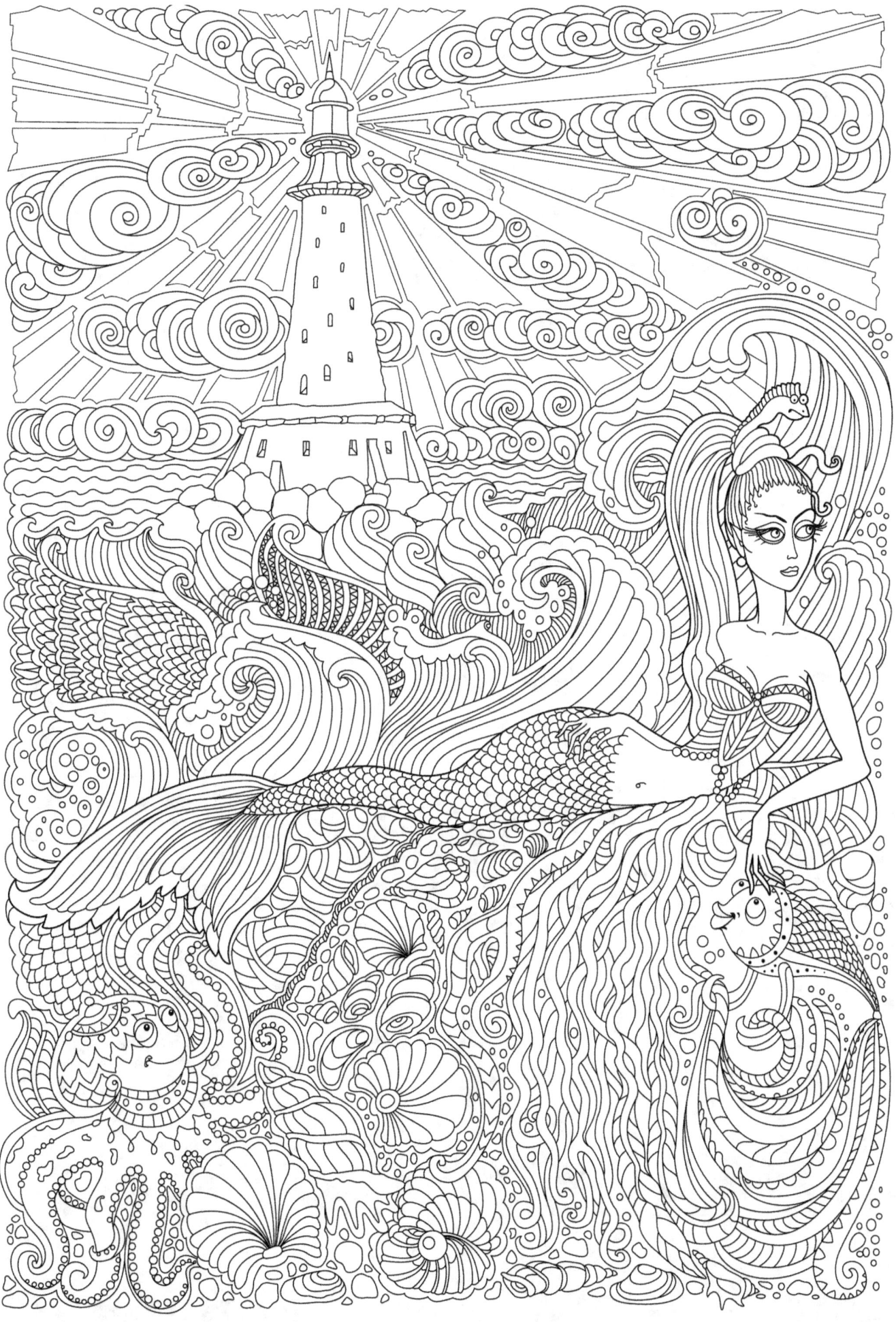

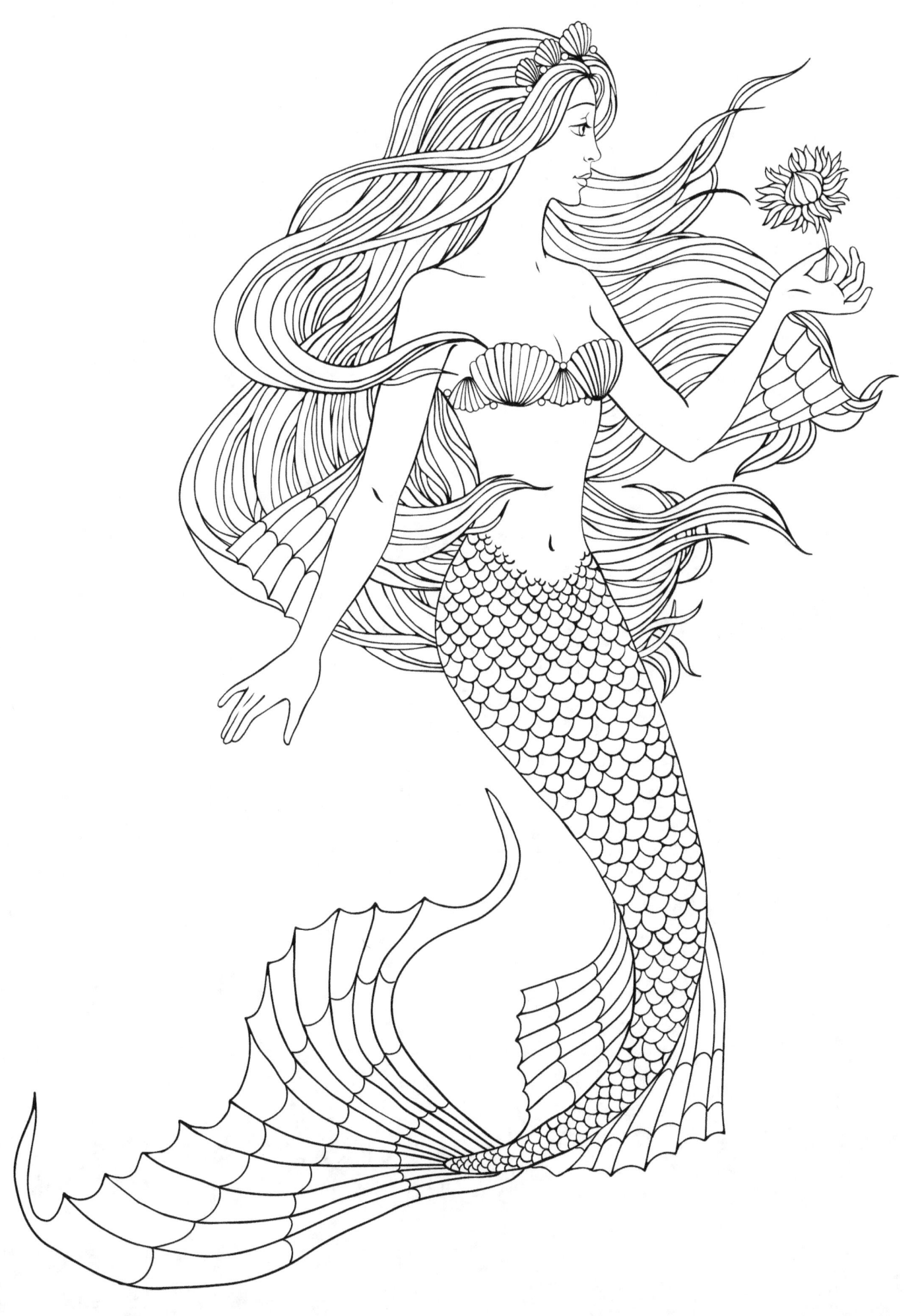

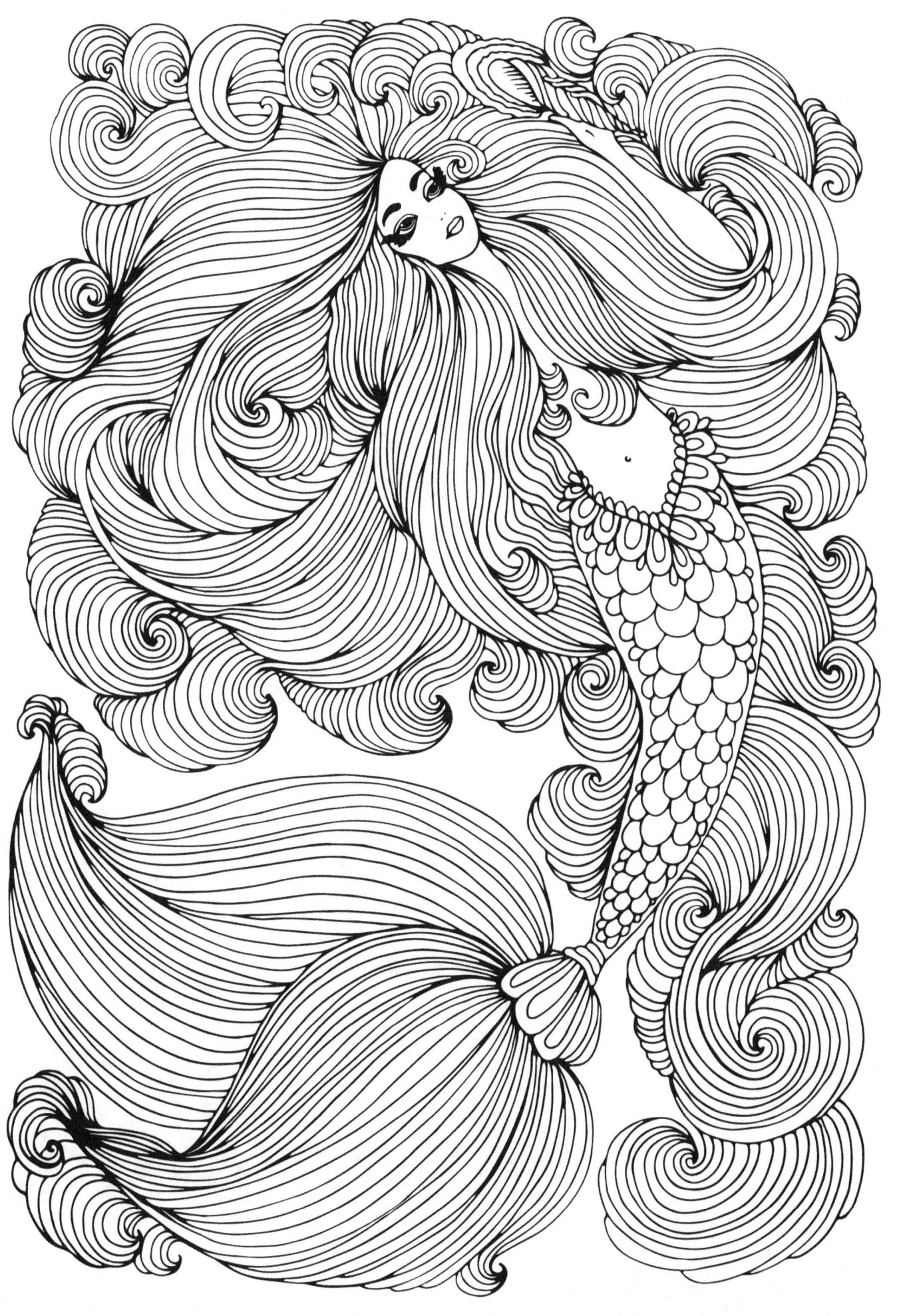

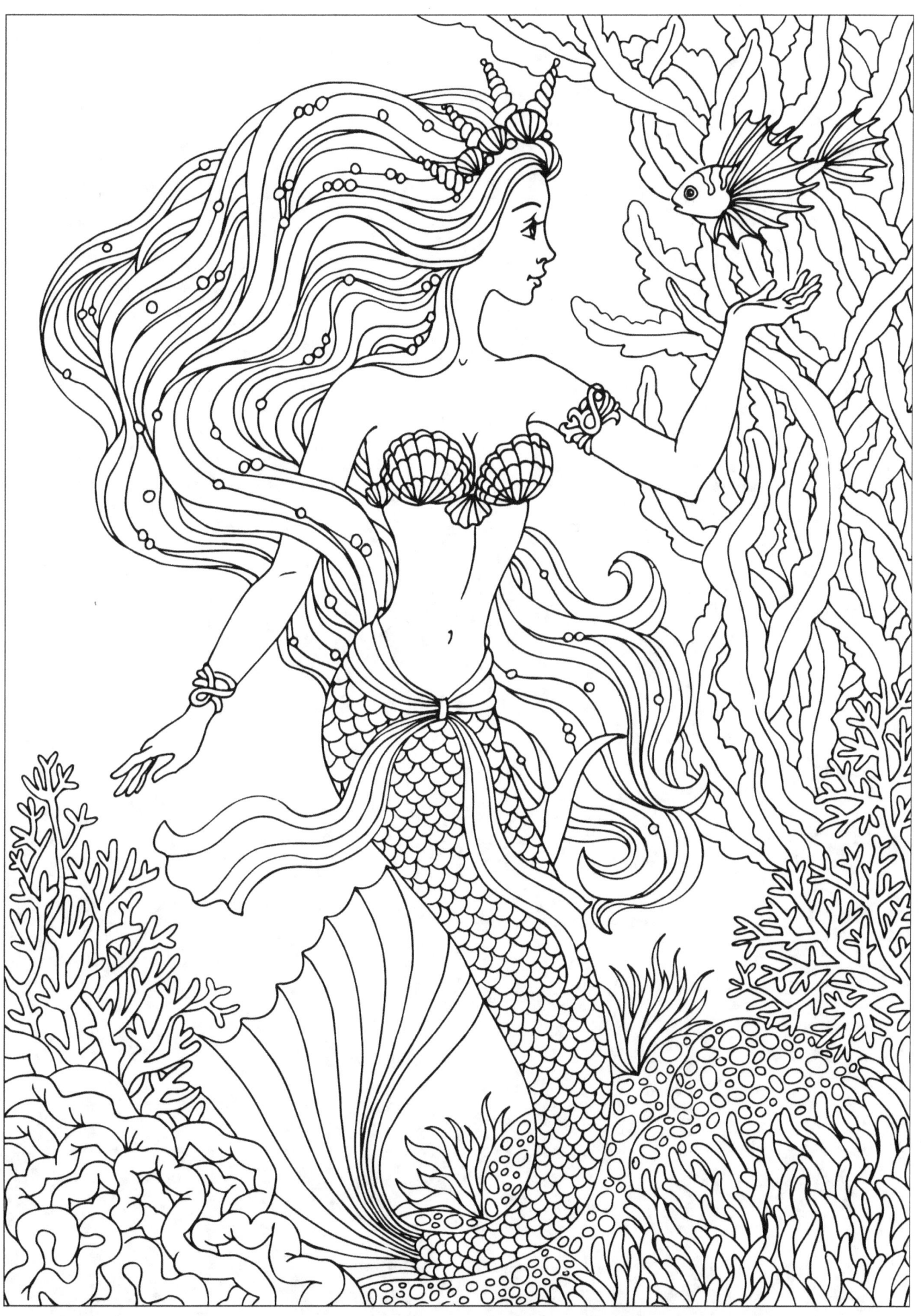

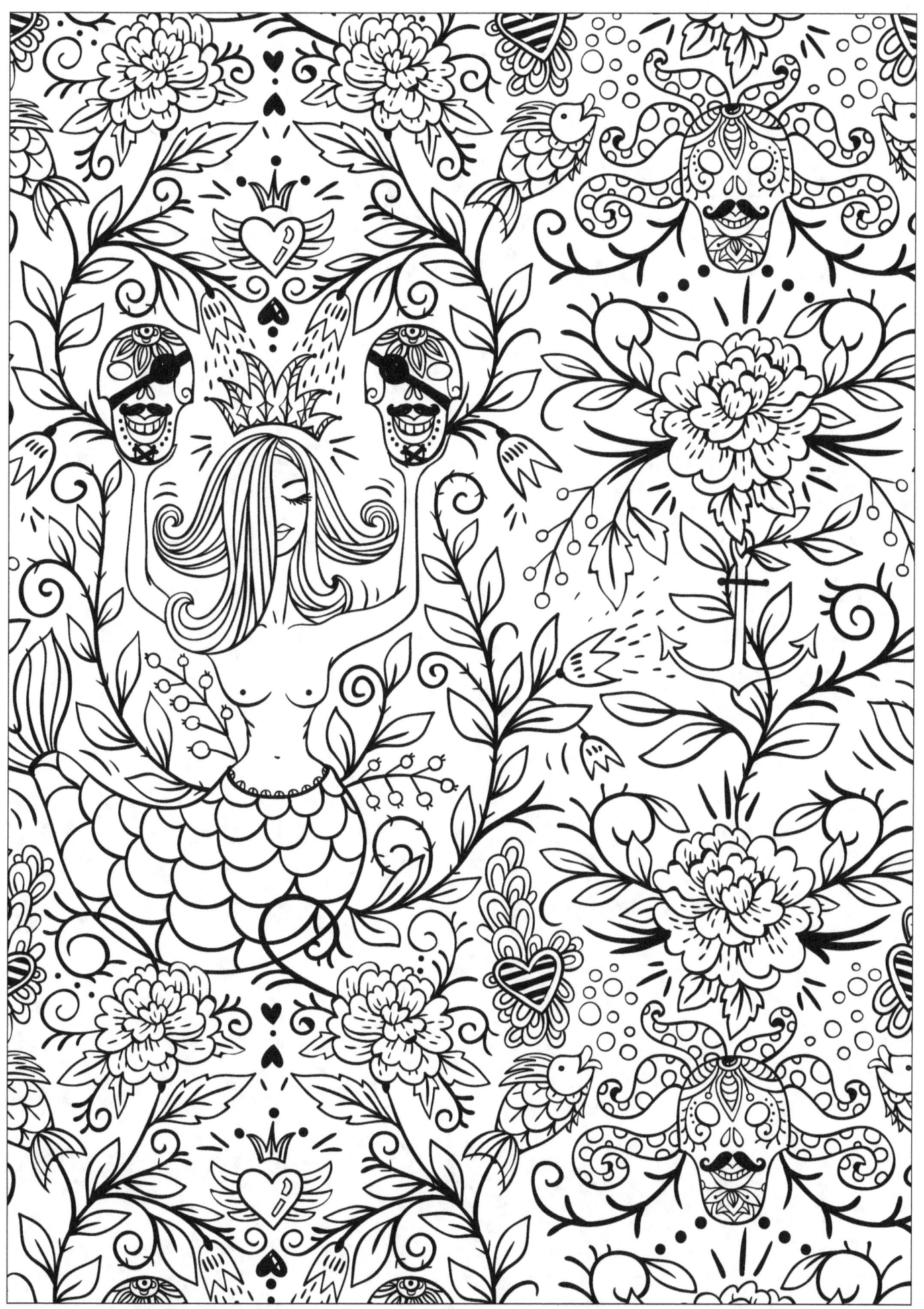

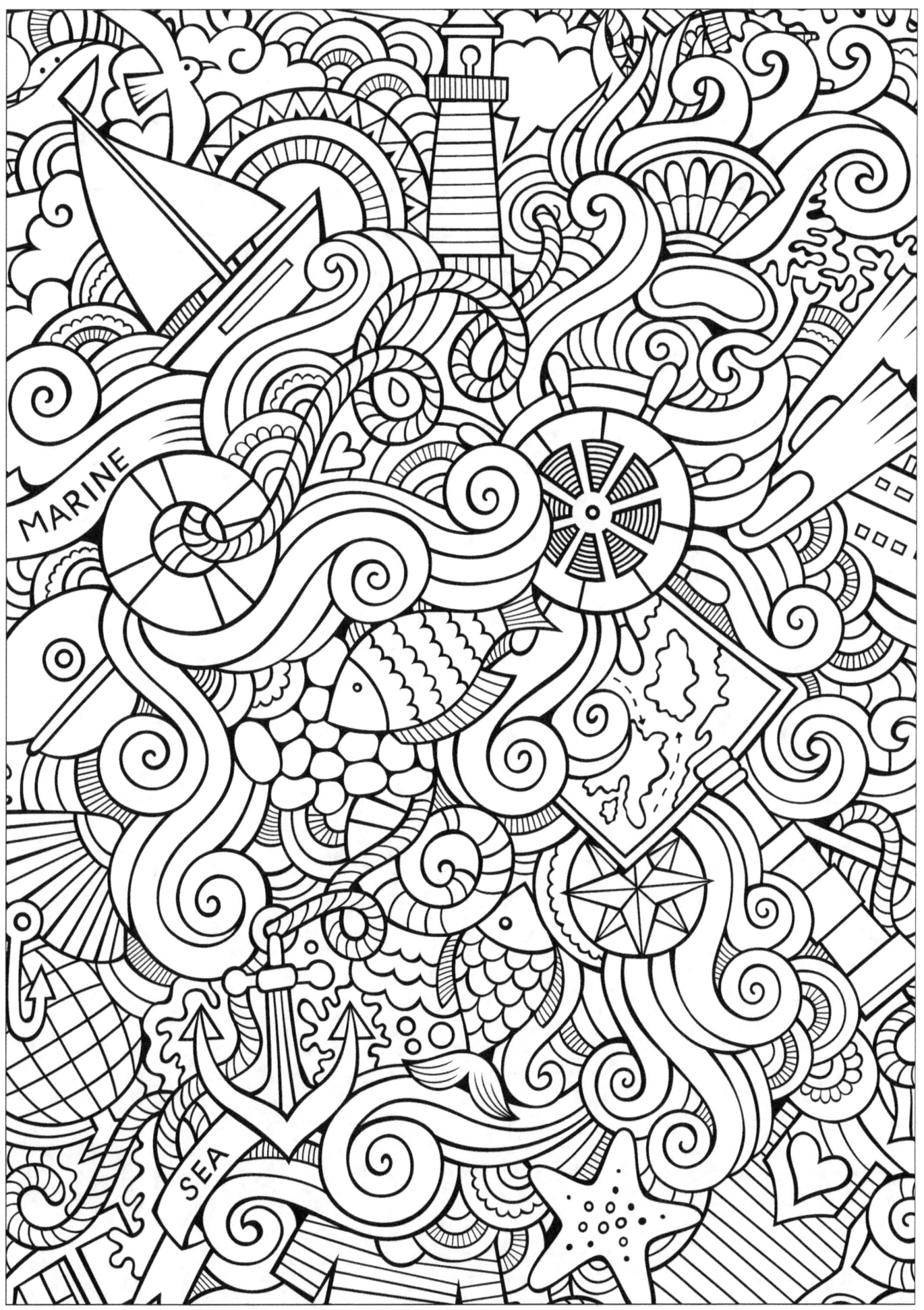

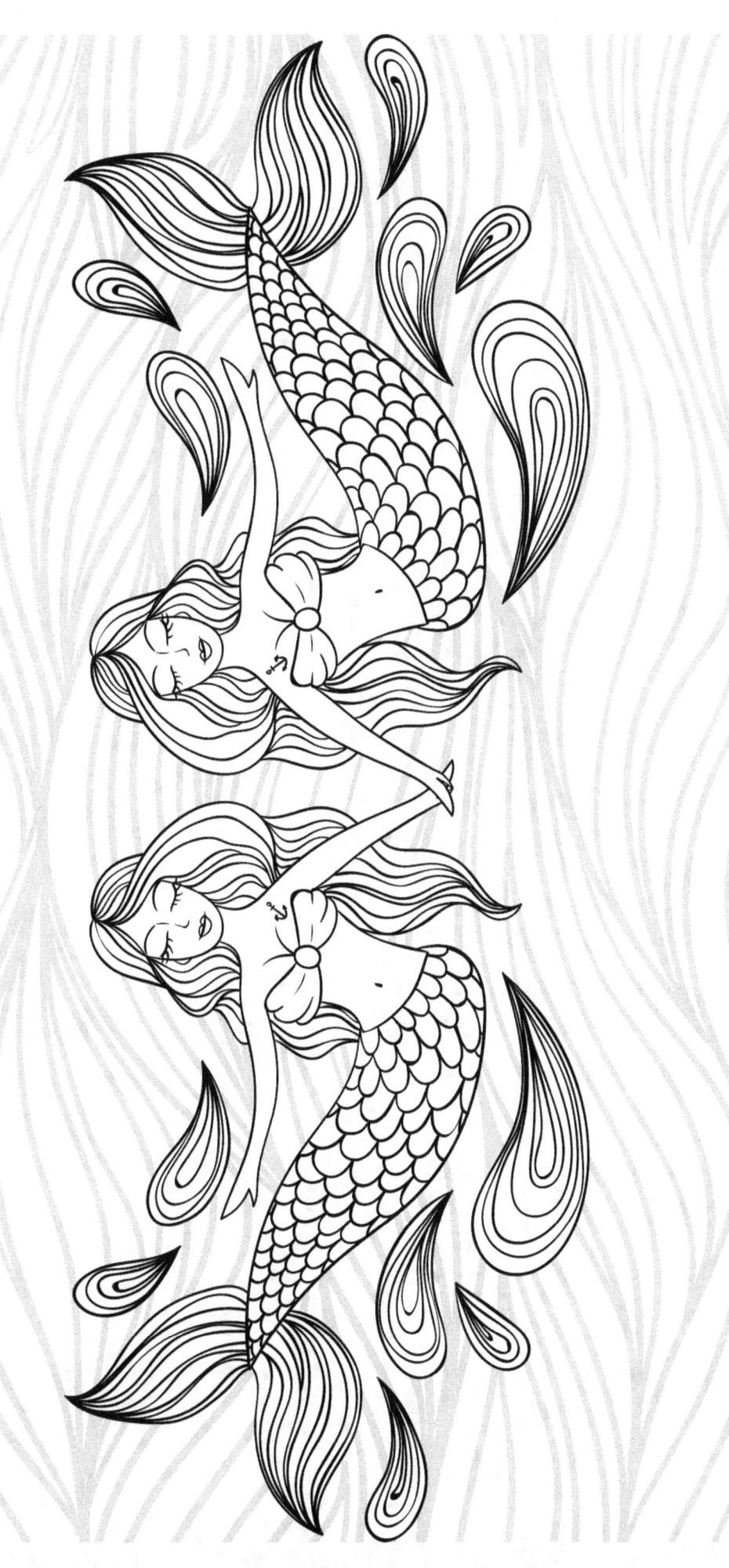

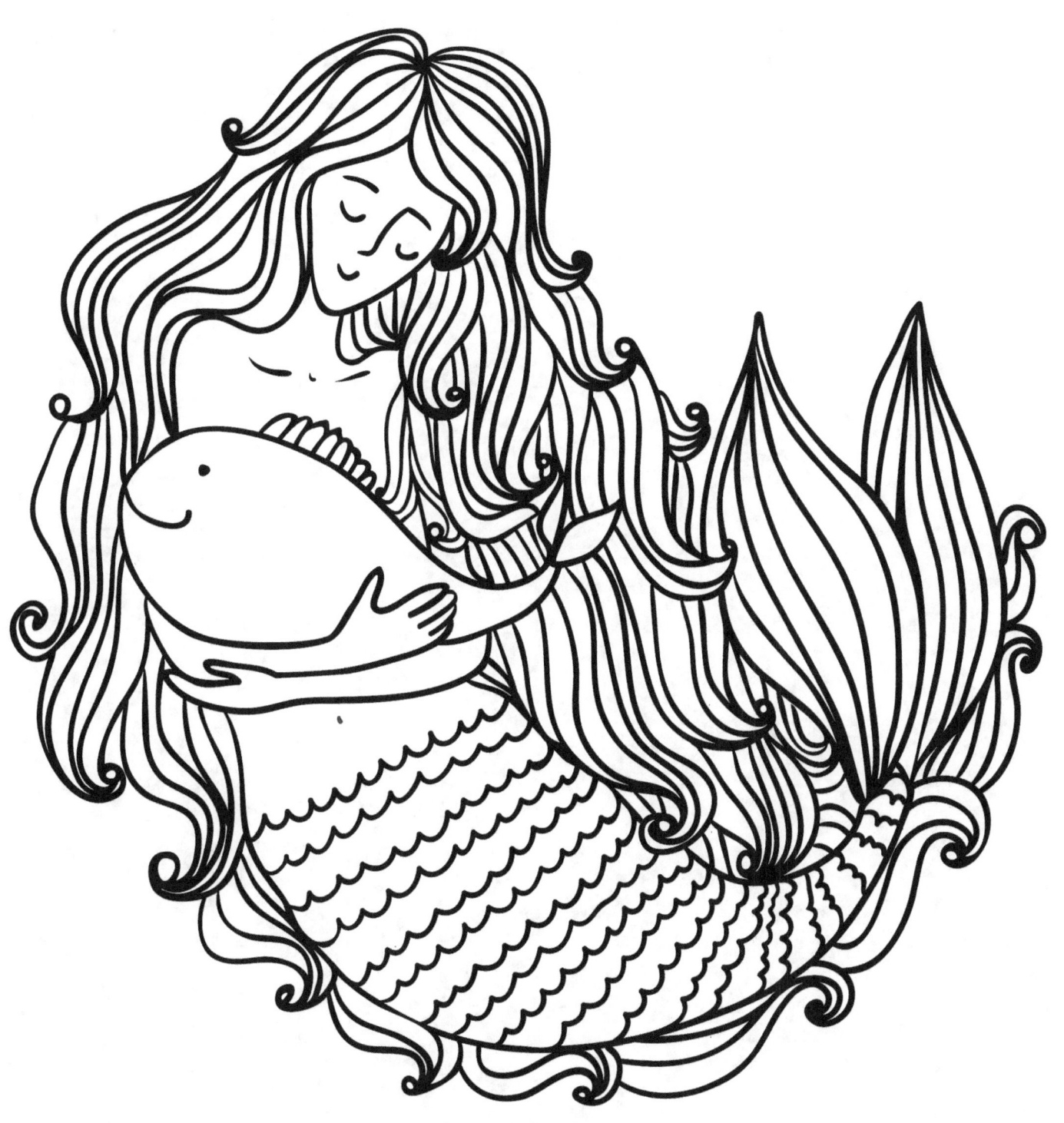

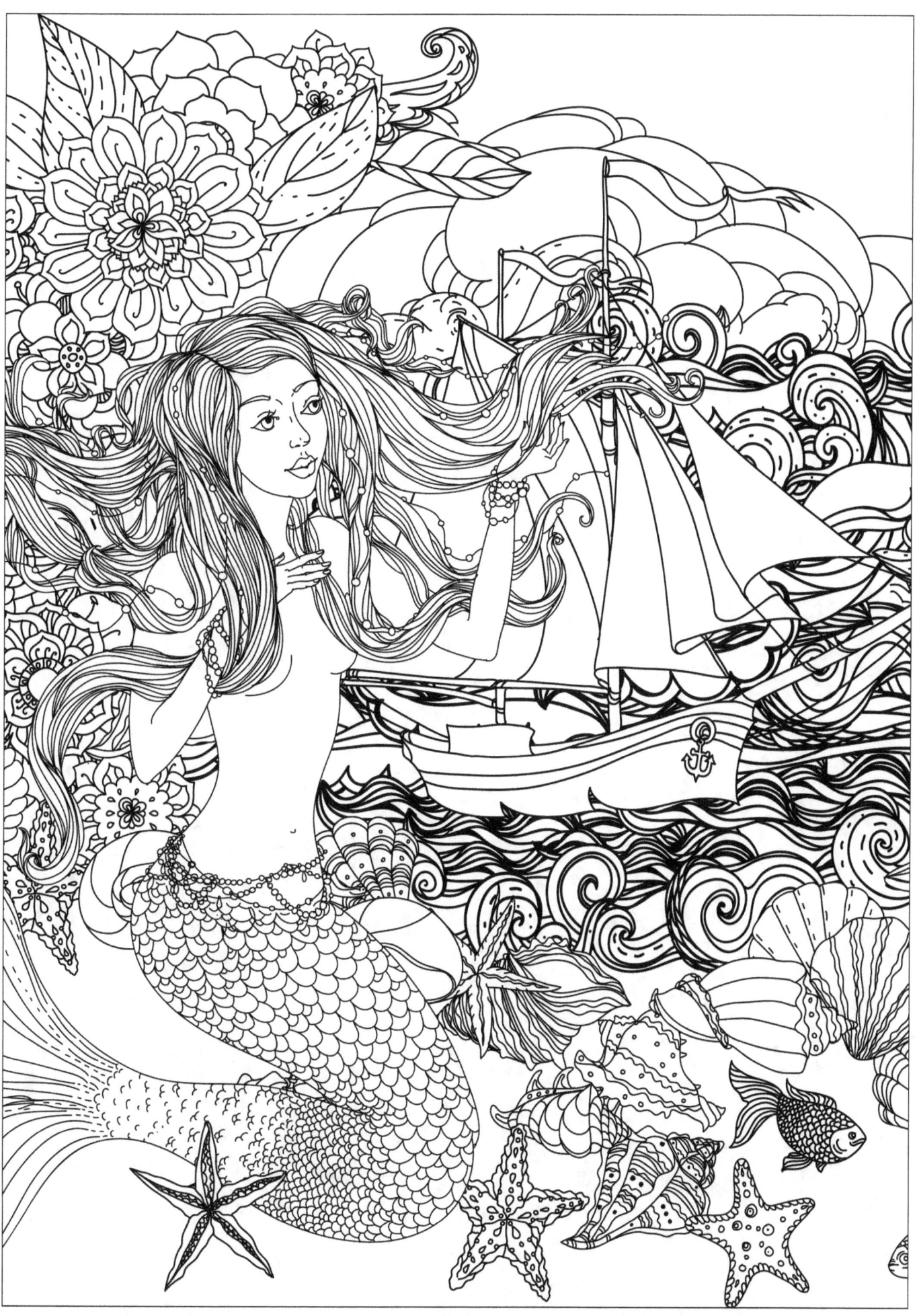

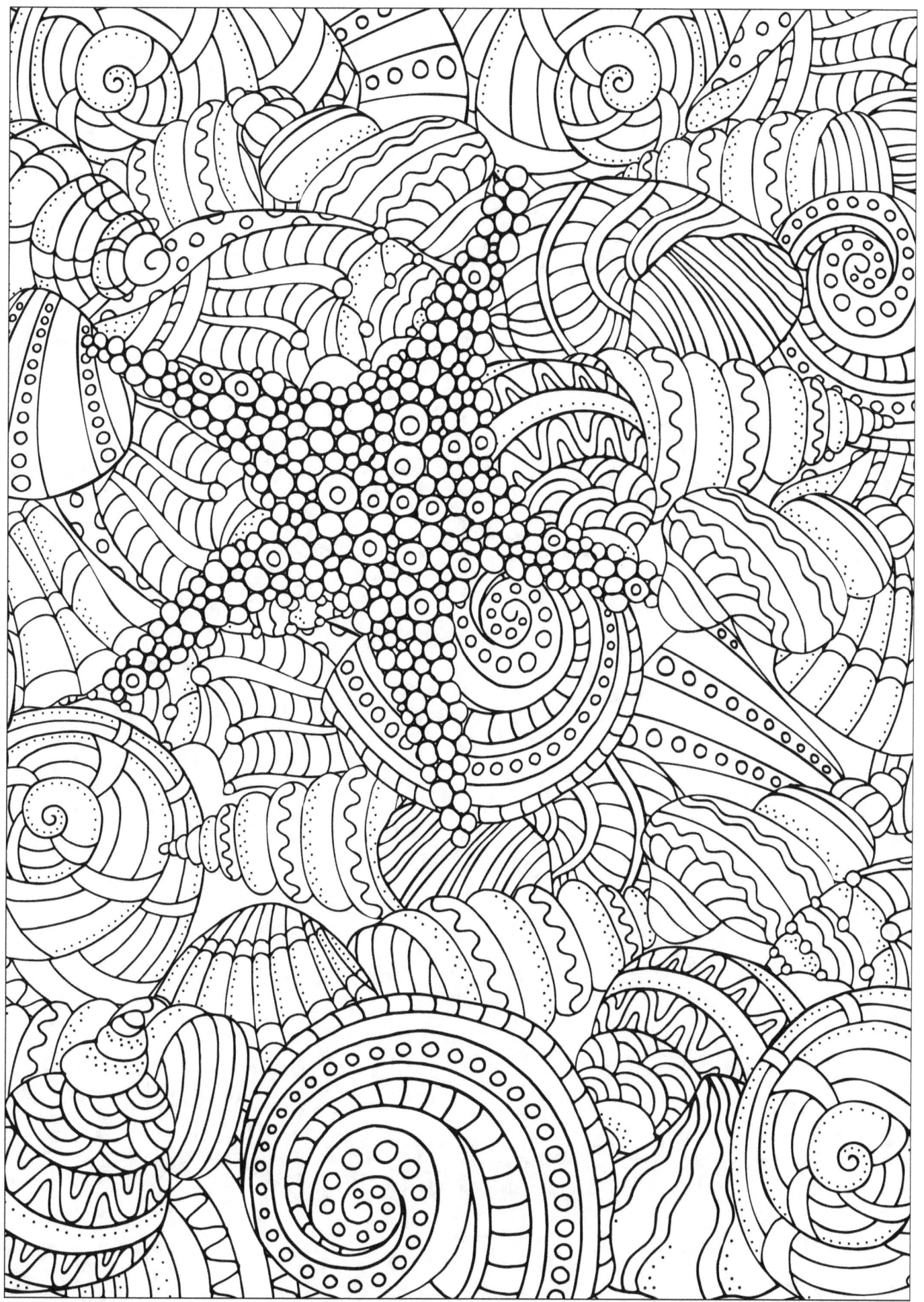

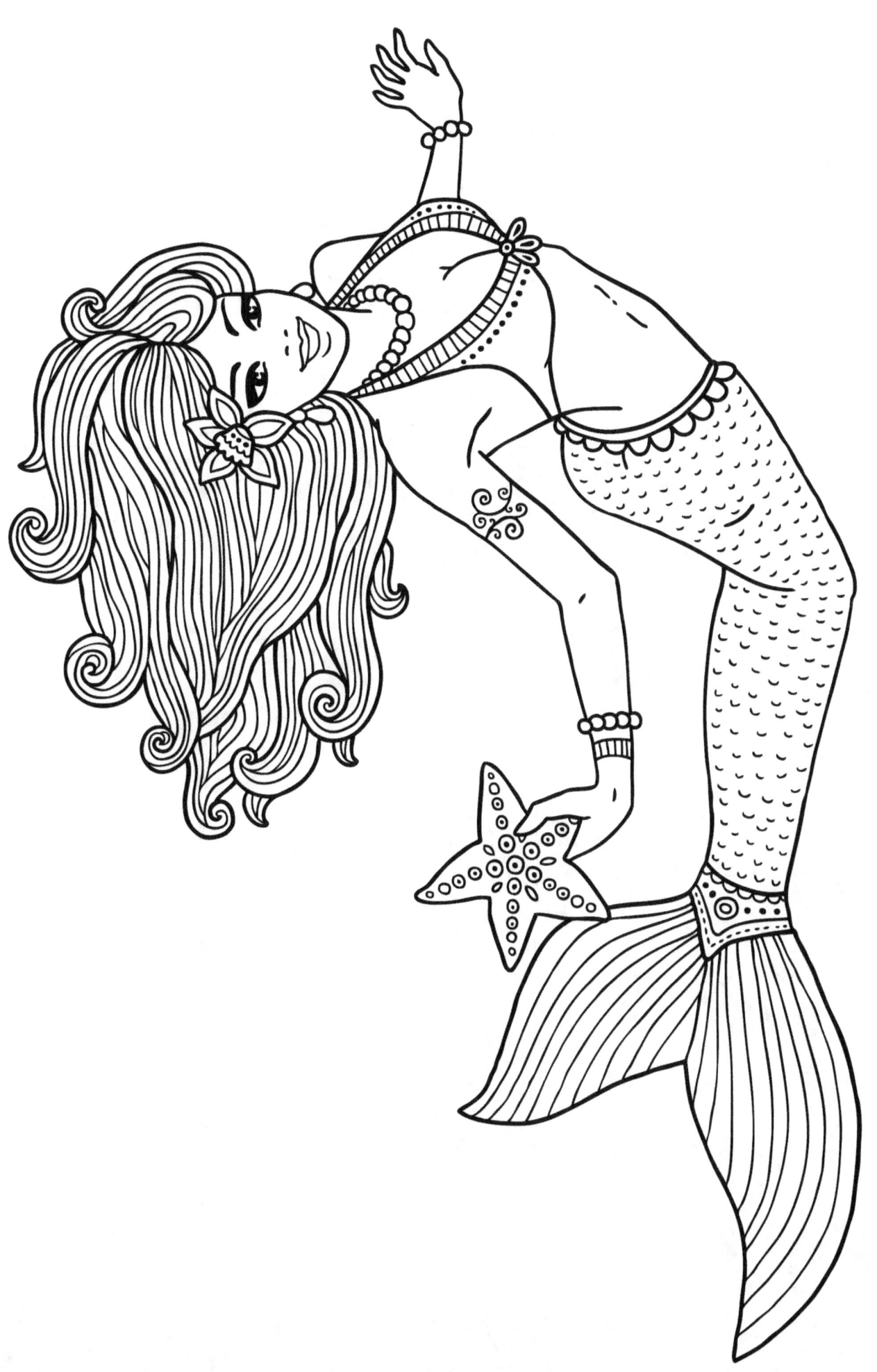

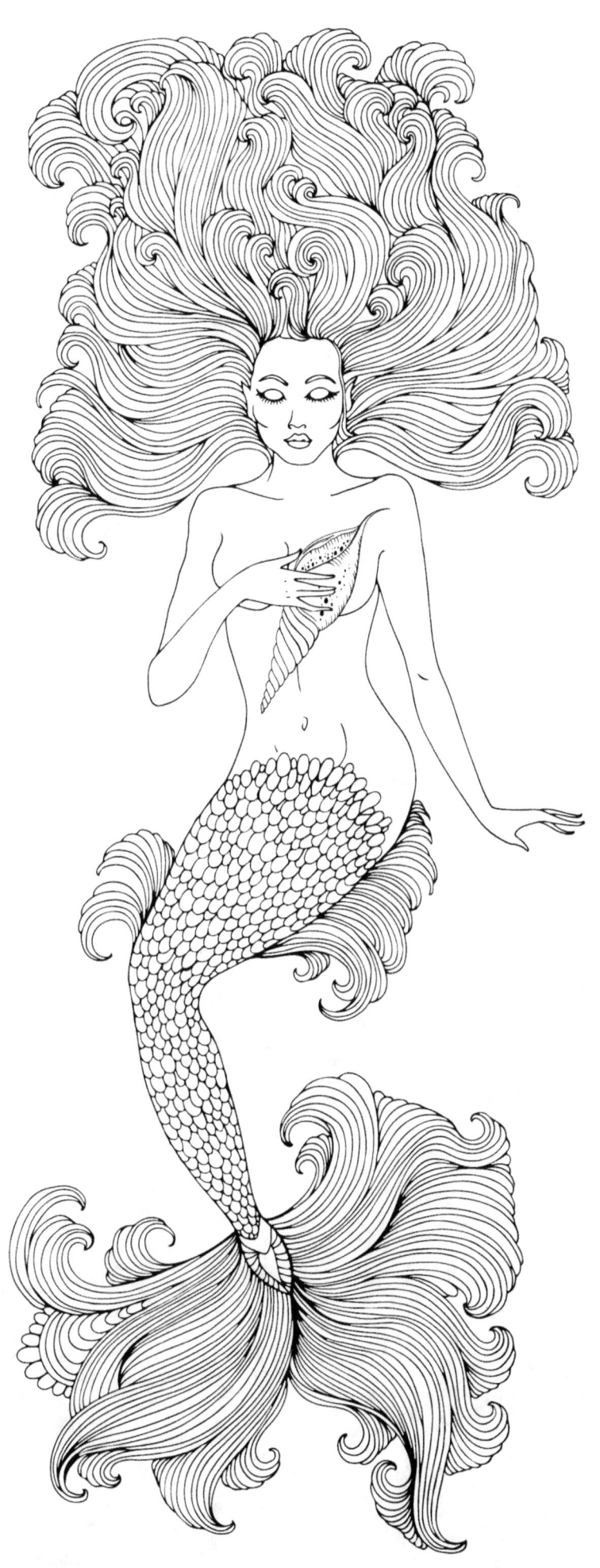

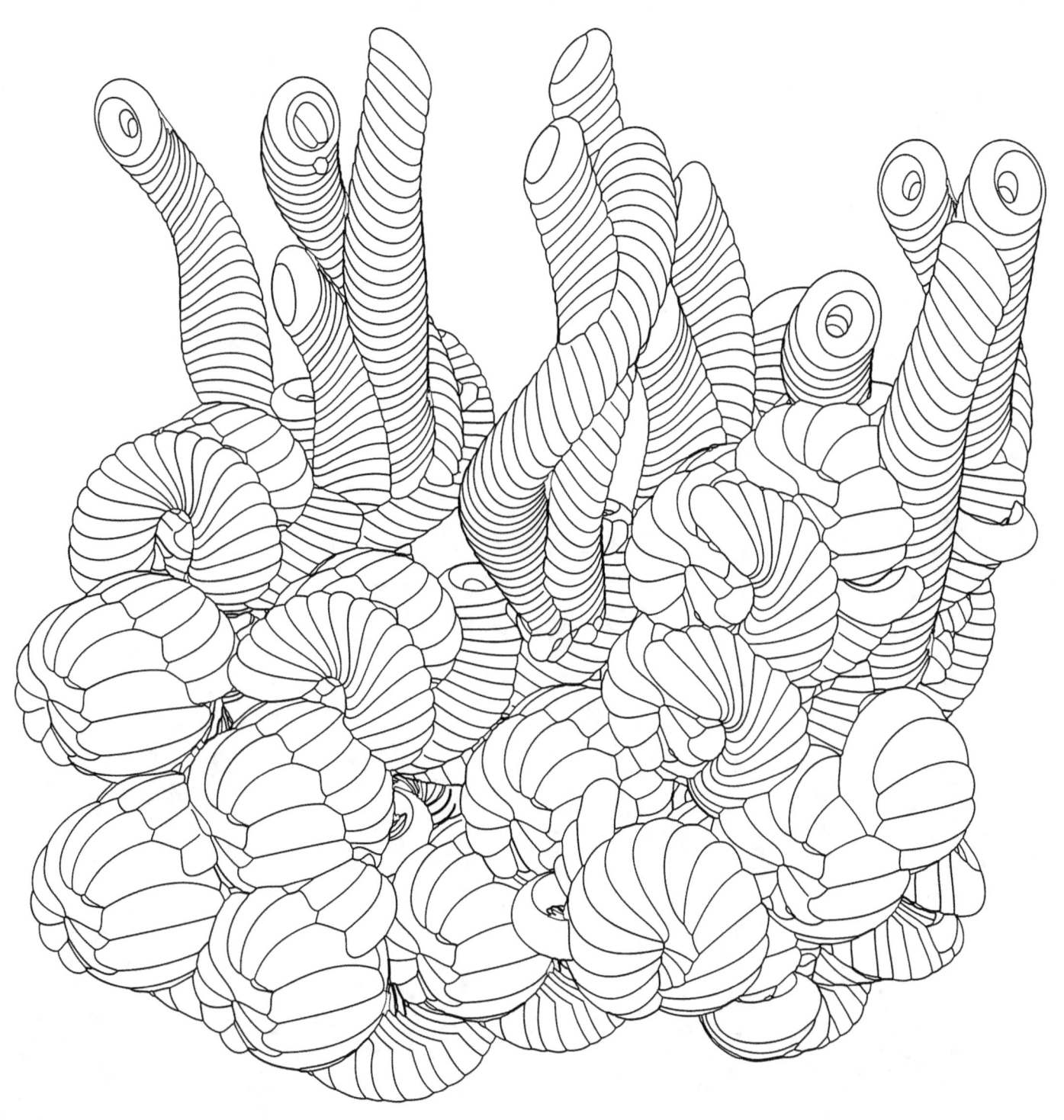

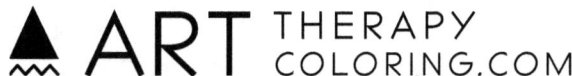

Test Your Colors

Drawings

Drawings

Best Selling Art Therapy Coloring Books

Coloring Books For Adults:

- Zombie Coloring Book: Black Background
- Butterfly Coloring Book For Adults: Black Background
- Tattoo Coloring Book: Black Background
- Coloring Books for Adults Relaxation: Native American Inspired Designs
- Fishing Coloring Book for Adults: Black Background

Coloring Books For Men:

- Coloring Book for Men: Anti-Stress Designs Vol 1
- Coloring Book For Men: Fishing Designs
- Coloring Book For Men: Tattoo Designs
- Coloring Books for Men: Hunting
- Coloring Book For Men: Biker Designs

Coloring Books For Seniors:

- Coloring Book For Seniors: Nature Designs Vol 1
- Coloring Book For Seniors: Anti-Stress Designs Vol 1
- Coloring Books for Seniors: Relaxing Designs
- Coloring Book For Seniors: Floral Designs Vol 1
- Coloring Book For Seniors: Ocean Designs Vol 1

Coloring Books For Teens and Tweens:

- Coloring Books For Teens: Ocean Designs
- Coloring Books for Teen Girls Vol 1
- Teen Inspirational Coloring Books
- Coloring Book for Teens: Anti-Stress Designs Vol 1
- Tween Coloring Books For Girls: Cute Animals

Coloring Books For Kids:

- Horse Coloring Book For Girls
- Coloring Books For Boys: Sharks
- Coloring Books for Boys: Animal Designs
- Unicorn Coloring Book for Girls
- Detailed Coloring Books For Kids

Art Therapy Coloring Books

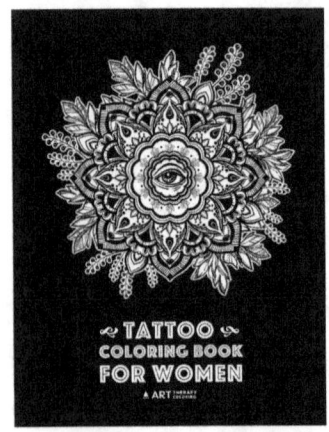

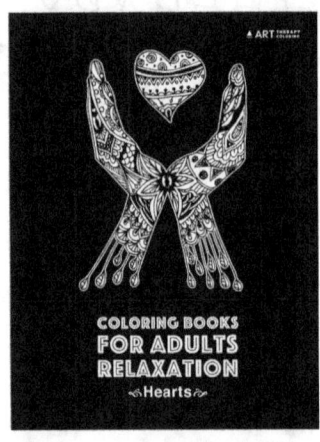

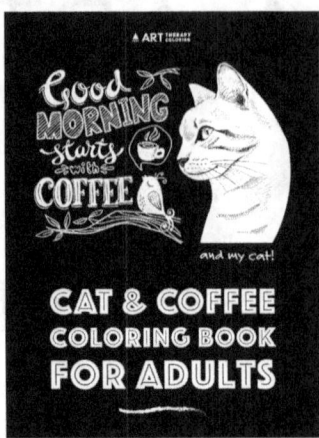

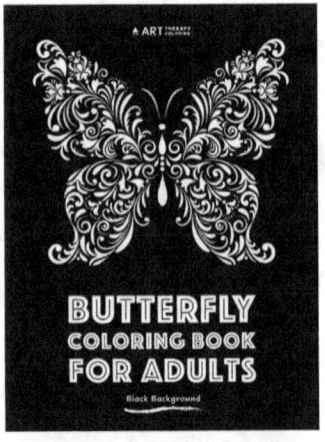

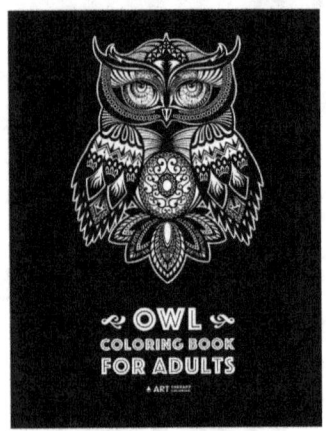

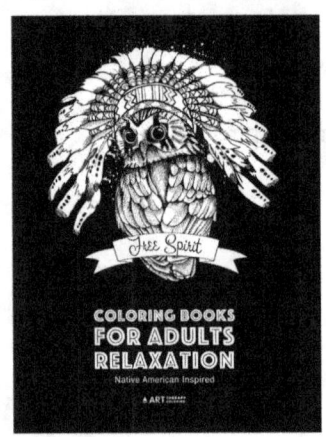

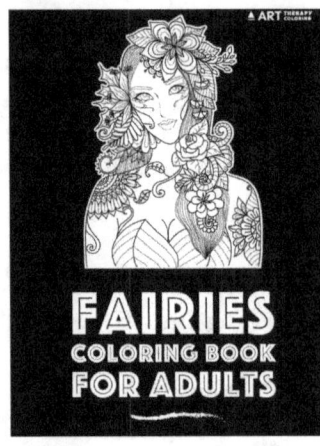

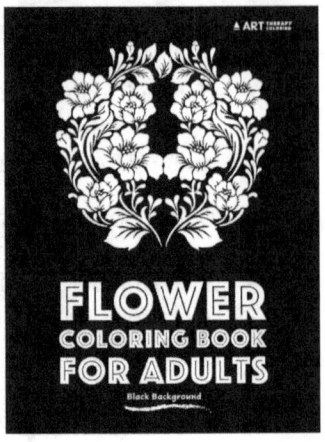

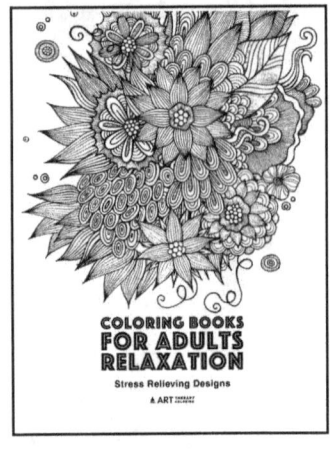

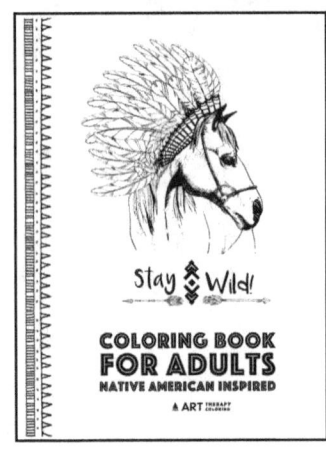

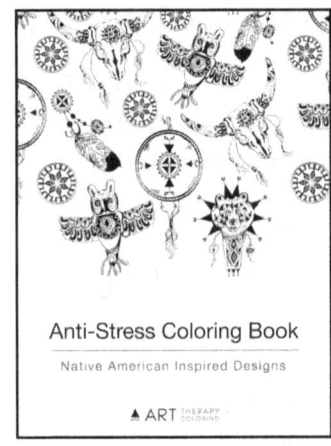

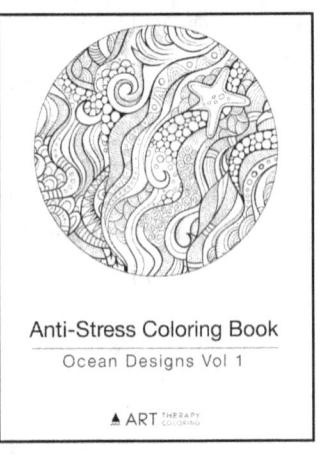

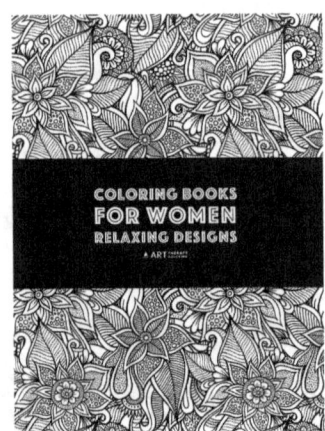

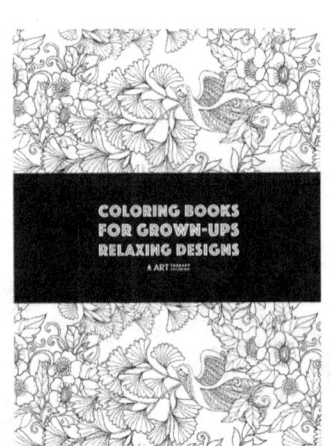

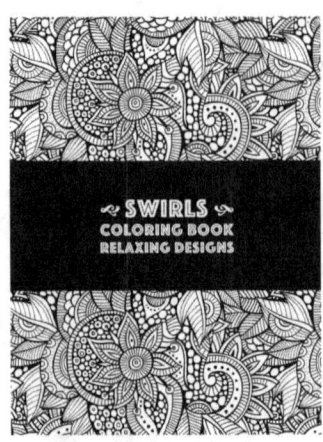

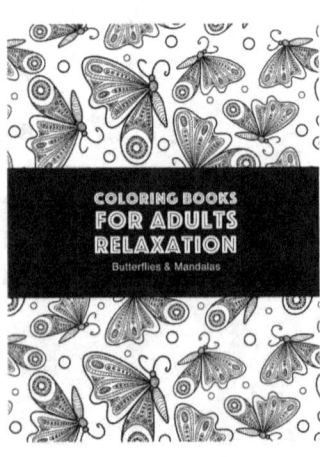

Art Therapy Coloring Books

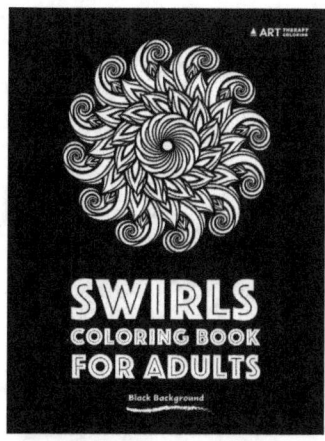

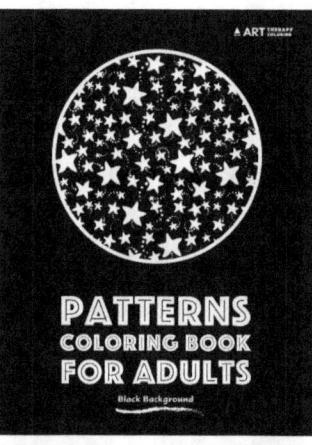

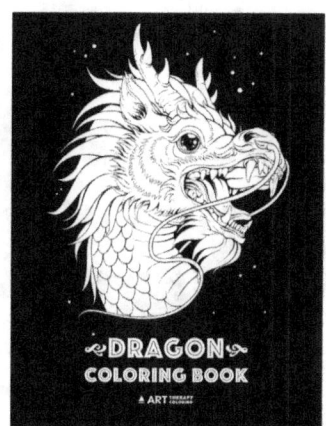

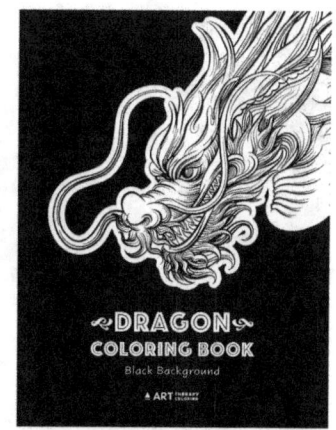

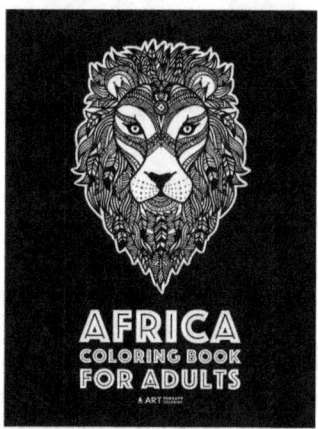

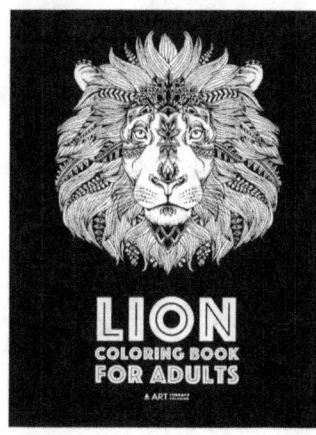

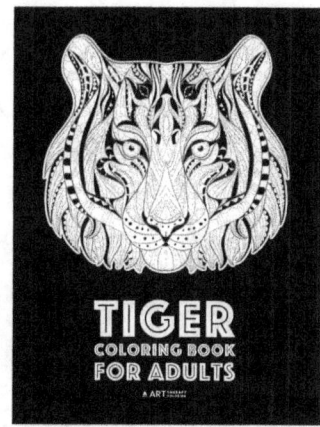

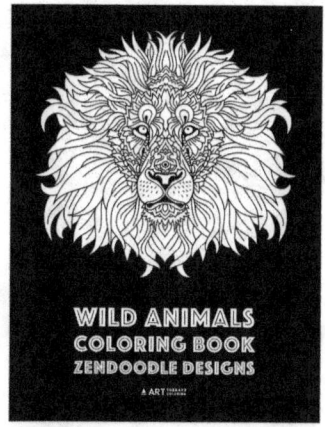

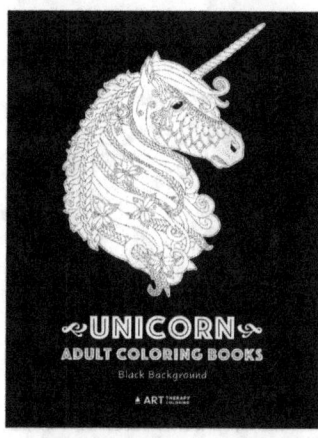

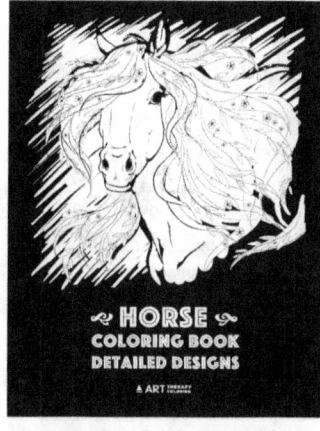

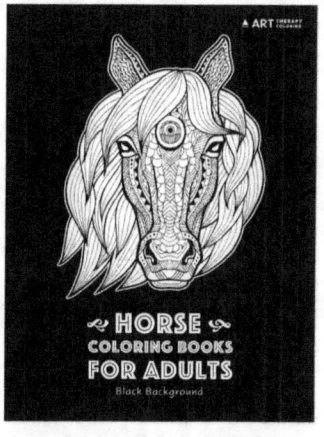

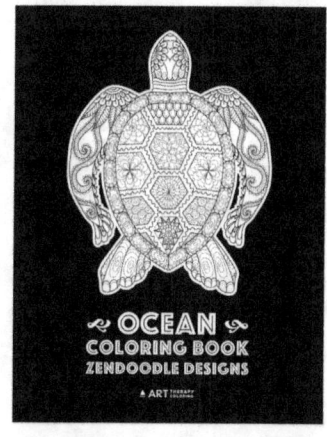

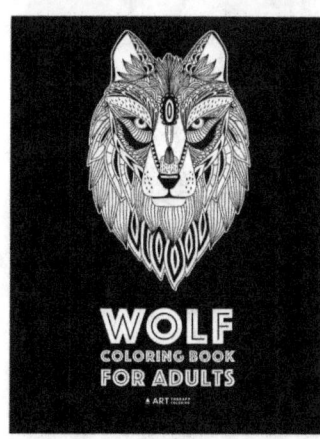

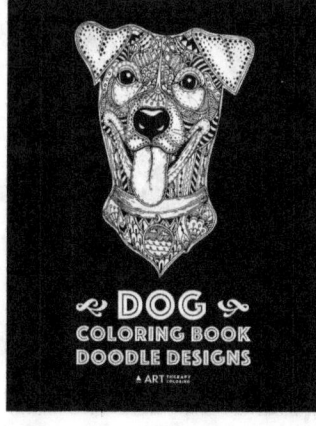

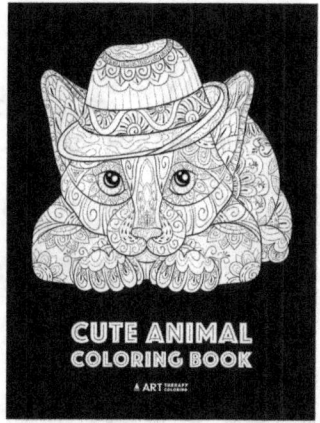

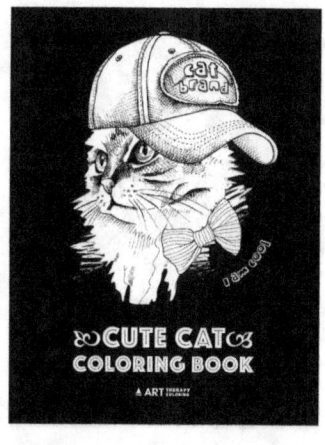

Art Therapy Coloring Books

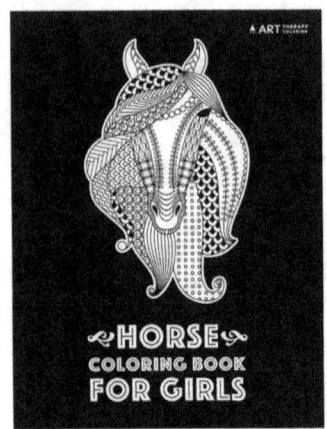

HORSE
COLORING BOOK
FOR GIRLS

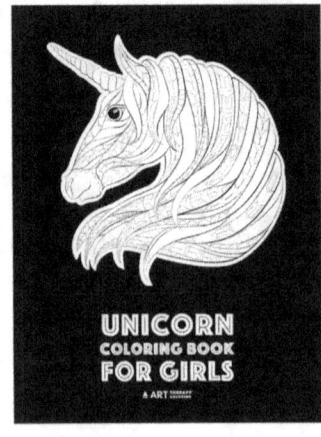

UNICORN
COLORING BOOK
FOR GIRLS

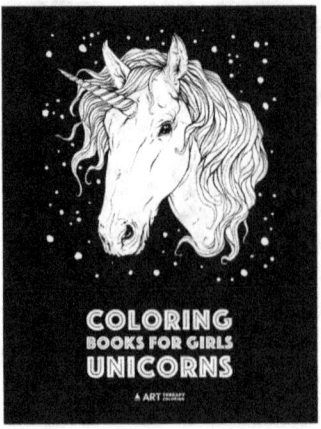

COLORING
BOOKS FOR GIRLS
UNICORNS

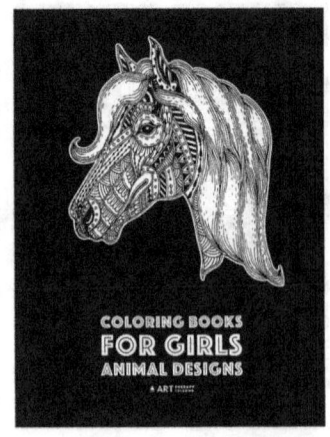

COLORING BOOKS
FOR GIRLS
ANIMAL DESIGNS

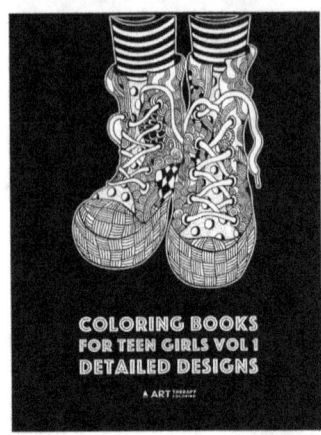

COLORING BOOKS
FOR TEEN GIRLS VOL 1
DETAILED DESIGNS

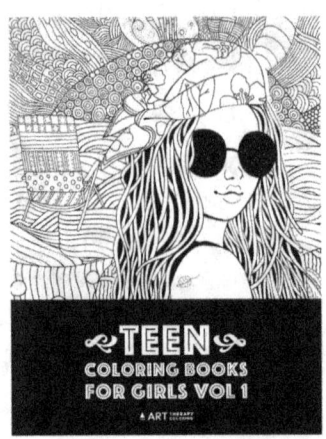

TEEN
COLORING BOOKS
FOR GIRLS VOL 1

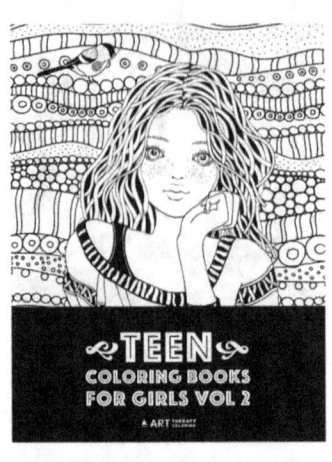

TEEN
COLORING BOOKS
FOR GIRLS VOL 2

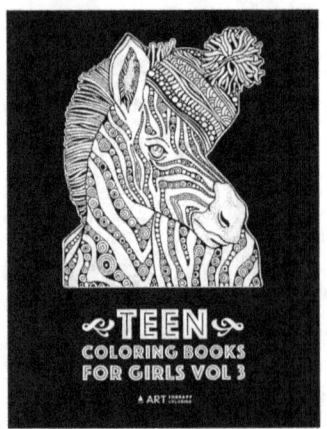

TEEN
COLORING BOOKS
FOR GIRLS VOL 3

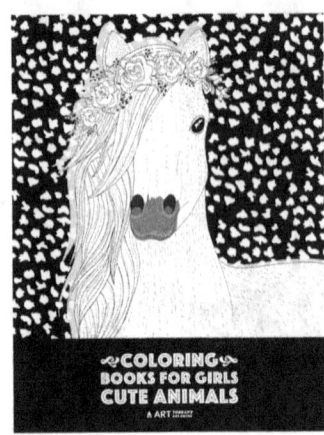

COLORING
BOOKS FOR GIRLS
CUTE ANIMALS

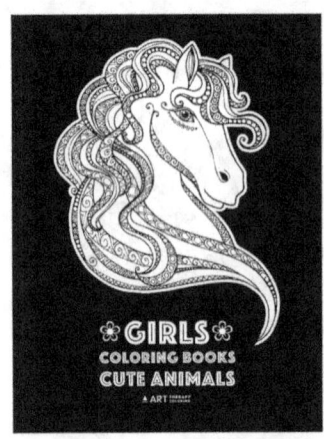

GIRLS
COLORING BOOKS
CUTE ANIMALS

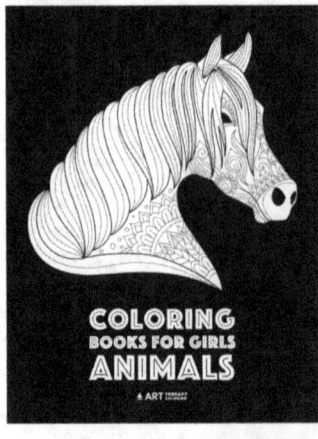

COLORING
BOOKS FOR GIRLS
ANIMALS

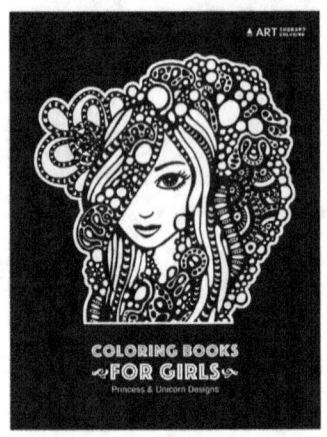

COLORING BOOKS
FOR GIRLS
Princess & Unicorn Designs

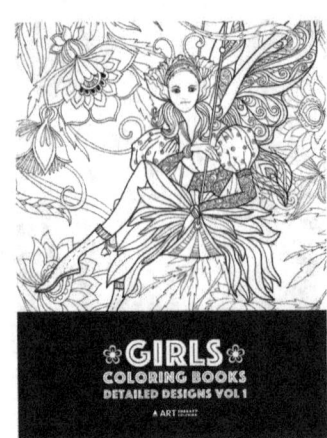

GIRLS
COLORING BOOKS
DETAILED DESIGNS VOL 1

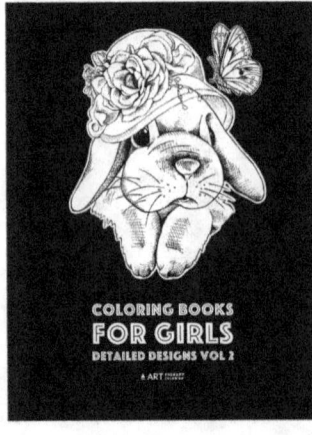

COLORING BOOKS
FOR GIRLS
DETAILED DESIGNS VOL 2

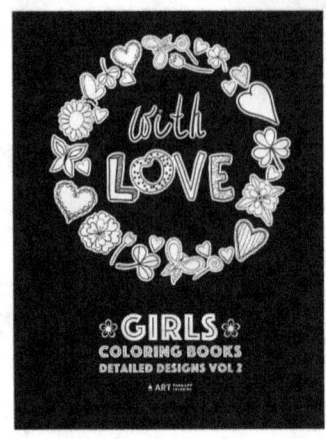

GIRLS
COLORING BOOKS
DETAILED DESIGNS VOL 2

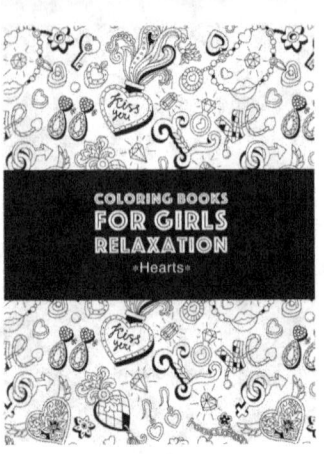

COLORING BOOKS
FOR GIRLS
RELAXATION
Hearts

Art Therapy Coloring Books

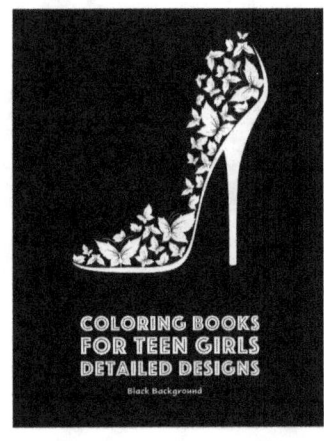

COLORING BOOKS
FOR TEEN GIRLS
DETAILED DESIGNS
Black Background

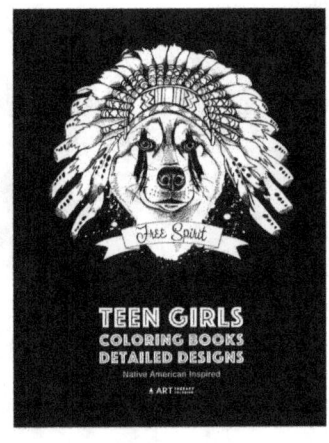

TEEN GIRLS
COLORING BOOKS
DETAILED DESIGNS
Native American Inspired

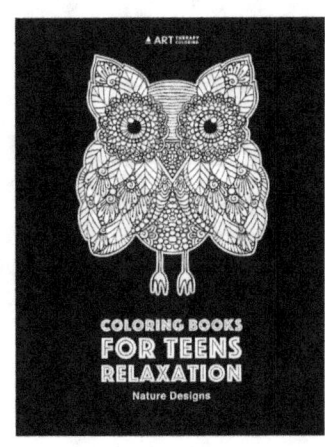

COLORING BOOKS
FOR TEENS
RELAXATION
Nature Designs

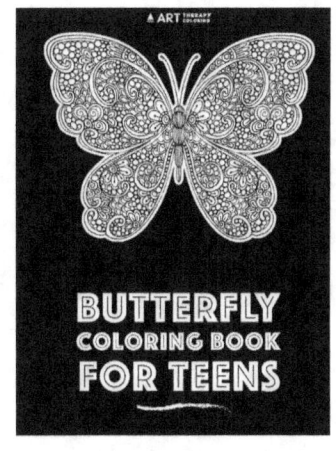

BUTTERFLY
COLORING BOOK
FOR TEENS

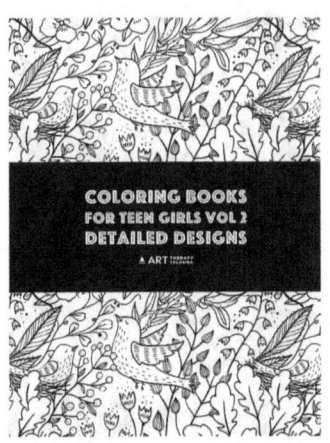

COLORING BOOKS
FOR TEEN GIRLS VOL 2
DETAILED DESIGNS

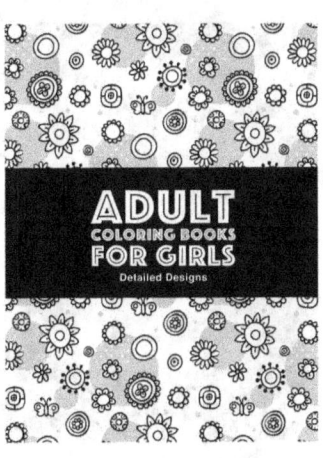

ADULT
COLORING BOOKS
FOR GIRLS
Detailed Designs

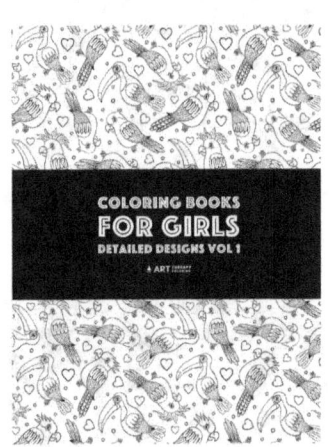

COLORING BOOKS
FOR GIRLS
DETAILED DESIGNS VOL 1

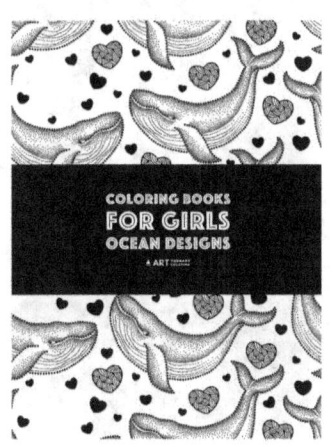

COLORING BOOKS
FOR GIRLS
OCEAN DESIGNS

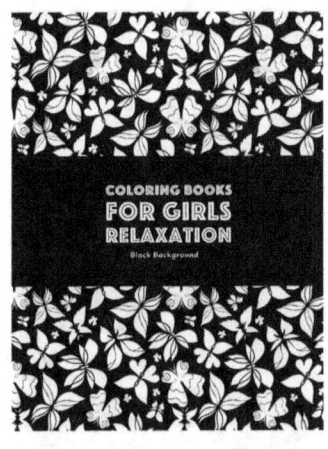

COLORING BOOKS
FOR GIRLS
RELAXATION
Black Background

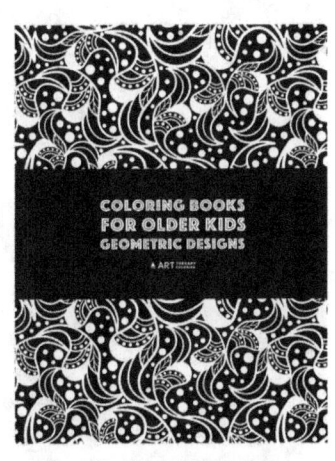

COLORING BOOKS
FOR OLDER KIDS
GEOMETRIC DESIGNS

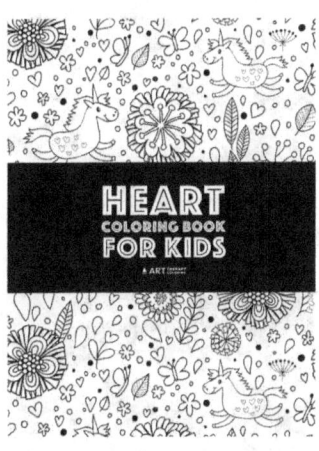

HEART
COLORING BOOK
FOR KIDS

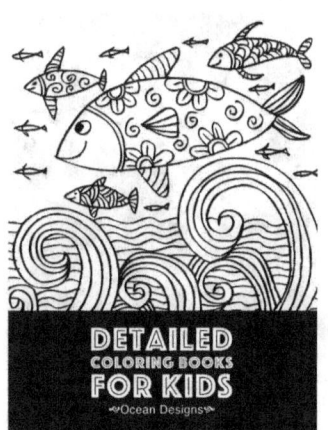

DETAILED
COLORING BOOKS
FOR KIDS
Ocean Designs

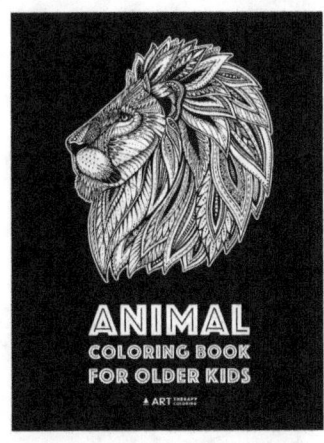

ANIMAL
COLORING BOOK
FOR OLDER KIDS

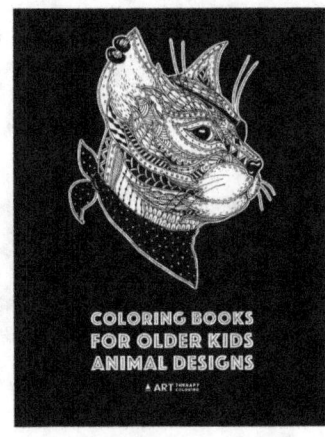

COLORING BOOKS
FOR OLDER KIDS
ANIMAL DESIGNS

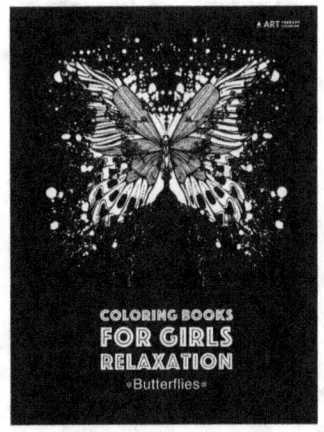

COLORING BOOKS
FOR GIRLS
RELAXATION
Butterflies

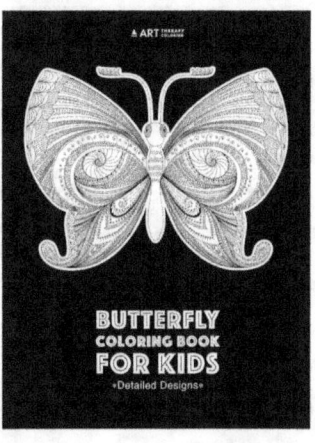

BUTTERFLY
COLORING BOOK
FOR KIDS
Detailed Designs

Art Therapy Coloring Books

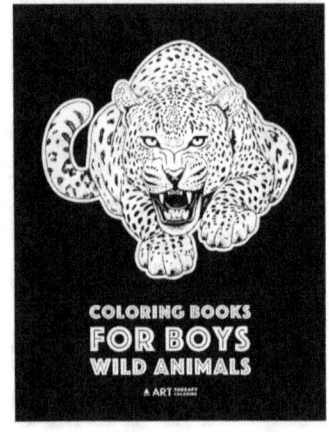

**COLORING BOOKS
FOR BOYS
WILD ANIMALS**

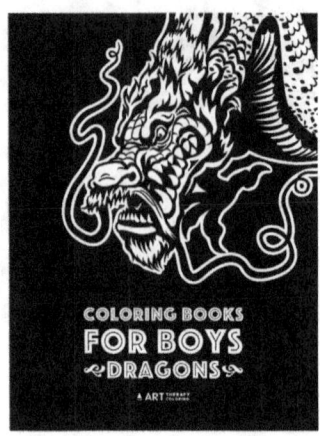

**COLORING BOOKS
FOR BOYS
DRAGONS**

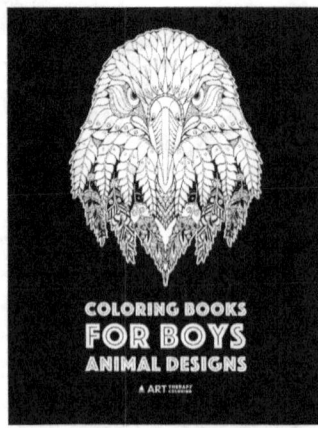

**COLORING BOOKS
FOR BOYS
ANIMAL DESIGNS**

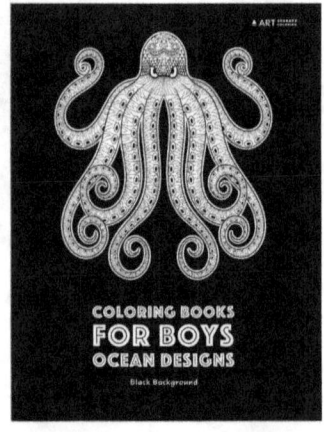

**COLORING BOOKS
FOR BOYS
OCEAN DESIGNS**
Black Background

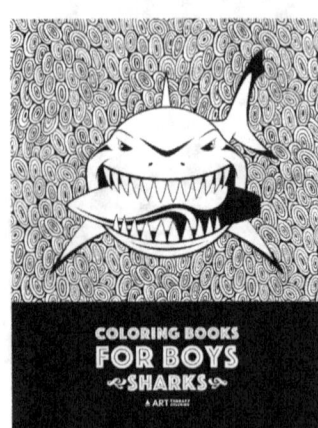

**COLORING BOOKS
FOR BOYS
SHARKS**

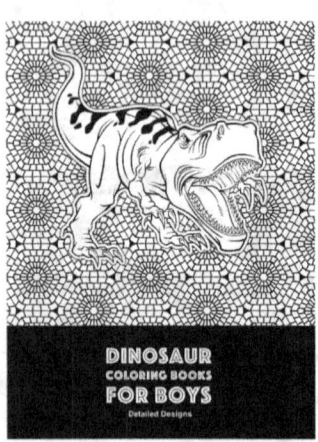

**DINOSAUR
COLORING BOOKS
FOR BOYS**
Detailed Designs

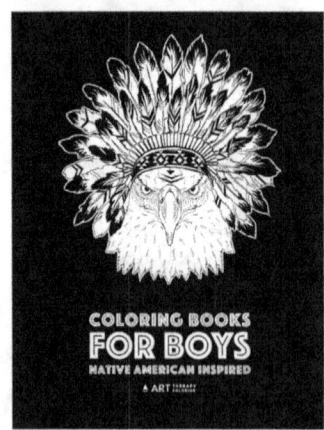

**COLORING BOOKS
FOR BOYS
NATIVE AMERICAN INSPIRED**

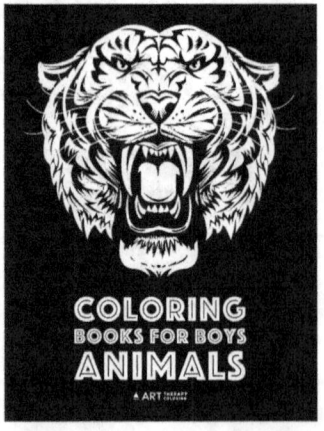

**COLORING
BOOKS FOR BOYS
ANIMALS**

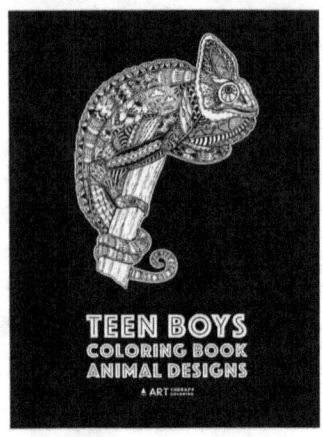

**TEEN BOYS
COLORING BOOK
ANIMAL DESIGNS**

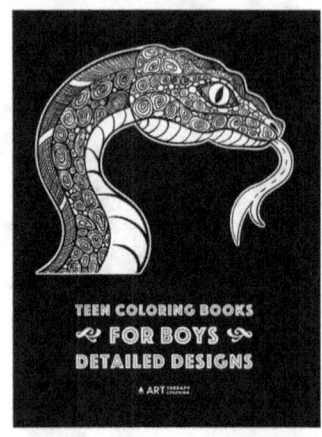

**TEEN COLORING BOOKS
FOR BOYS
DETAILED DESIGNS**

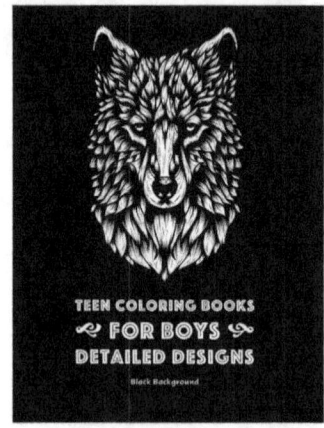

**TEEN COLORING BOOKS
FOR BOYS
DETAILED DESIGNS**
Black Background

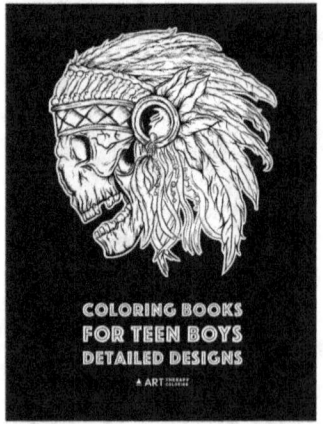

**COLORING BOOKS
FOR TEEN BOYS
DETAILED DESIGNS**

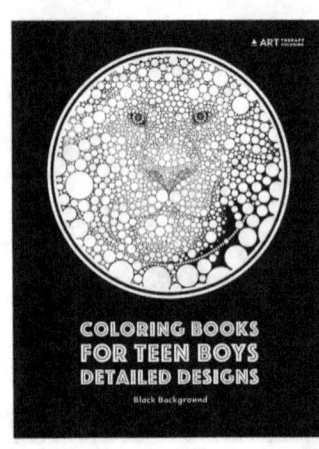

**COLORING BOOKS
FOR TEEN BOYS
DETAILED DESIGNS**
Black Background

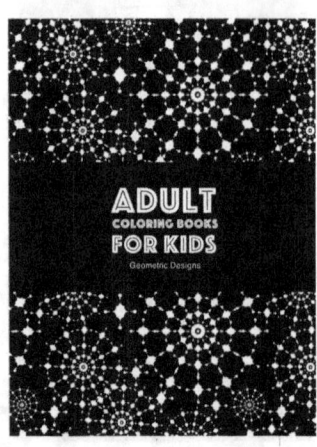

**ADULT
COLORING BOOKS
FOR KIDS**
Geometric Designs

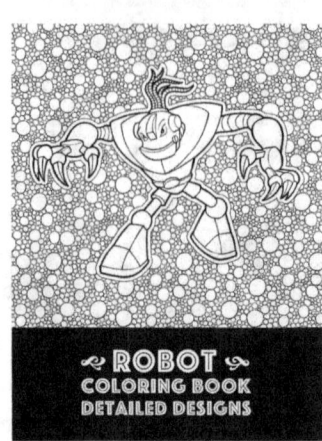

**ROBOT
COLORING BOOK
DETAILED DESIGNS**

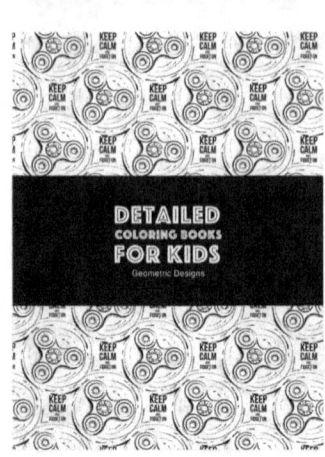

**DETAILED
COLORING BOOKS
FOR KIDS**
Geometric Designs

Art Therapy Coloring Books

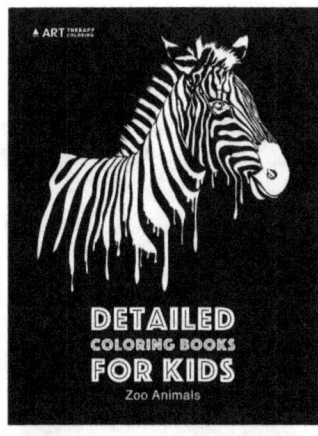

DETAILED
COLORING BOOKS
FOR KIDS
Zoo Animals

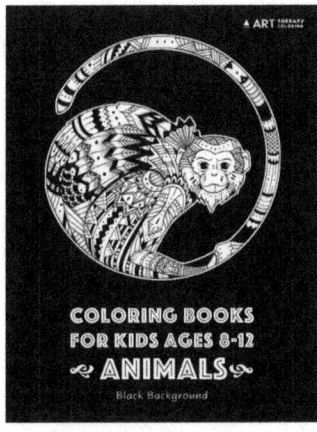

COLORING BOOKS
FOR KIDS AGES 8-12
ANIMALS
Black Background

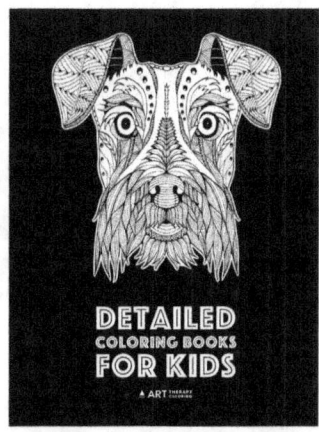

DETAILED
COLORING BOOKS
FOR KIDS

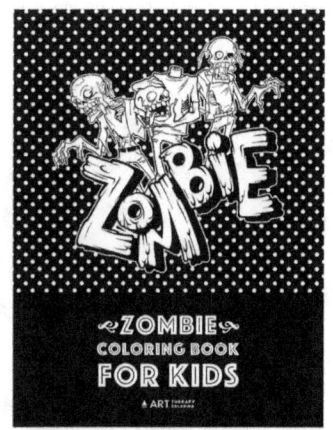

ZOMBIE
COLORING BOOK
FOR KIDS

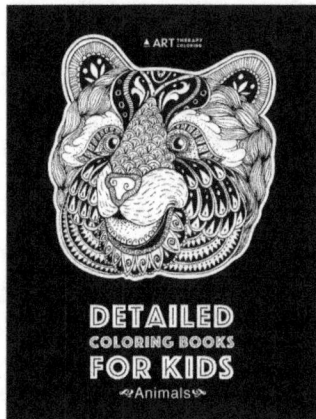

DETAILED
COLORING BOOKS
FOR KIDS
Animals

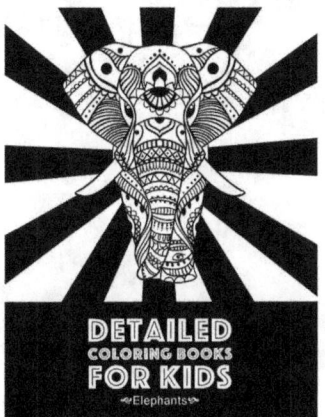

DETAILED
COLORING BOOKS
FOR KIDS
Elephants

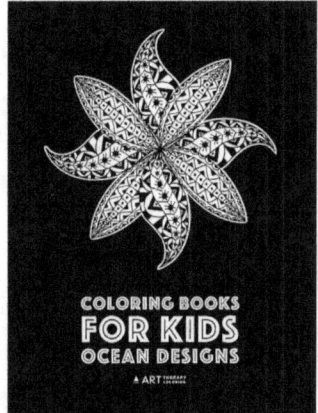

COLORING BOOKS
FOR KIDS
OCEAN DESIGNS

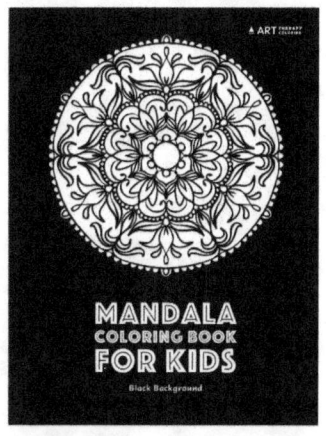

MANDALA
COLORING BOOK
FOR KIDS
Black Background

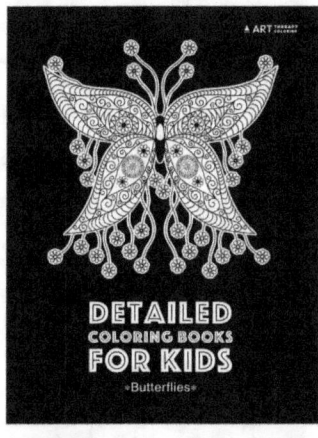

DETAILED
COLORING BOOKS
FOR KIDS
Butterflies

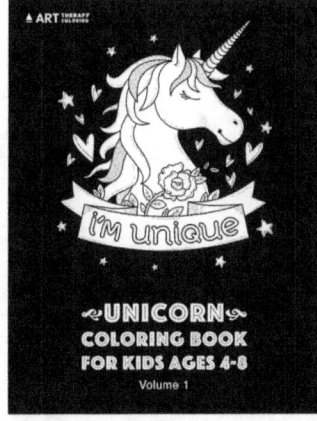

UNICORN
COLORING BOOK
FOR KIDS AGES 4-8
Volume 1

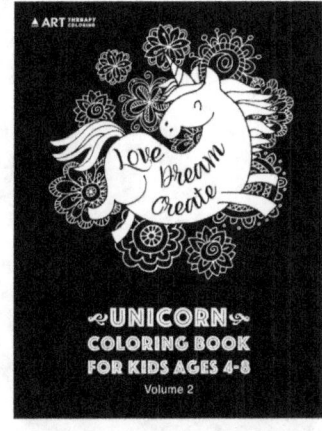

UNICORN
COLORING BOOK
FOR KIDS AGES 4-8
Volume 2

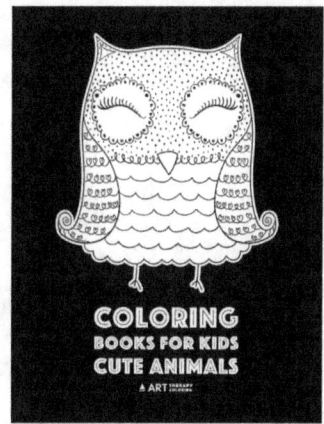

COLORING
BOOKS FOR KIDS
CUTE ANIMALS

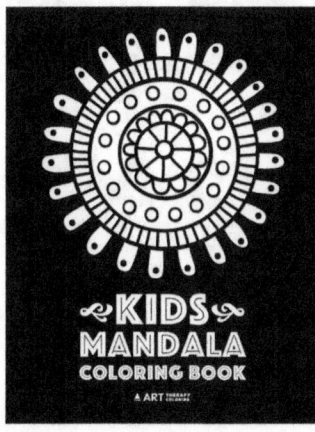

**KIDS
MANDALA**
Coloring Book

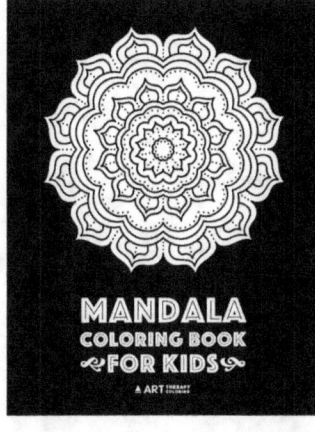

MANDALA
COLORING BOOK
FOR KIDS

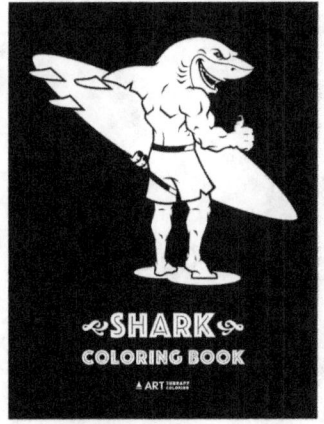

SHARK
COLORING BOOK

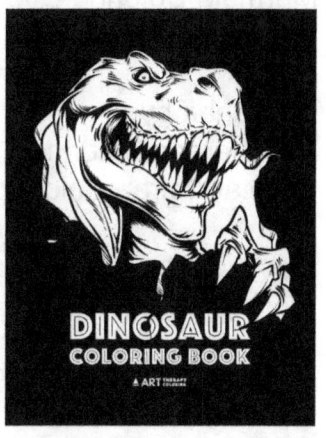

DINOSAUR
COLORING BOOK

Mermaid Coloring Book
For Adults

Published by:
Art Therapy Coloring
www.arttherapycoloring.com

ISBN: 978-1-944427-98-6